WHAT OTHEF

Rabbi Barney Kasdan's new commentary on Paul's (Rabbi Shaul's) letter to the Ephesians is a valuable addition to biblical commentaries written from a Messianic Jewish perspective. Years of study and life experience as the leader of a Messianic Jewish community have equipped him to write a commentary that is biblically sound and locates Rabbi Shaul in his Jewish world, even as the "apostle to the Gentiles."
—Akiva Cohen, Ph.D., Tel Aviv University

Barney Kasdan offers a new and refreshing perspective on the letter of Paul to the Ephesians. His commentary brings the reader back to the Jewish context in which Sha'ul and the early believers in Yeshua lived their new-found faith. His integration of rabbinic literature adds clarity and depth to the discussion. A fascinating and thought-provoking resource for Jewish and Gentile believers alike!
—Dr. Hélène Dellaire, Professor of Old Testament & Director of Messianic Judaism Programs, Denver Seminary

Writing in his usual plain and straightforward style, he provides the vital, missing dimension of a Messianic Jewish vantage point on Paul. Integrating the often-ignored rabbinic sources with significant exegetical insights, as well as important religious, cultural, and historical information, Rabbi Kasdan has made a valuable contribution to the study of the Epistles.
—Rabbi Dr. John Fischer
Vice President of Academics, St. Petersburg Seminary and Yeshiva

Rabbi Kasdan brings clarity to the texts of Shaul's writings, giving them their correct context, as part and parcel of the diverse 1st century Jewish world. His exposition of Paul's points upholds the integrity of Paul's thought, while emphasizing the very needed Jewish backgrounds to Paul's thought process. Very readable and well done.
—Rabbi Dr. D. Friedman, Jerusalem, Israel

Rabbi Barney Kasdan has very effectively captured the Jewish historical background of Ephesians in an accurate and winsome way. Mishnaic and Talmudic references add significant detail. Controversial issues in the Messianic movement are handled with firm conviction and gentle persuasion. All believers who read this book will find highly beneficial applications to today.
—Gregory Hagg, Ph.D.
Professor: Talbot School of Theology
Director: The Charles L. Feinberg Center or Messianic Jewish Studies

I am very pleased to commend this new commentary from Barney Kasdan. It is a worthy contribution to that important trend in scholarship to see the writings of the New Testament in their original Jewish context.
—Dr. Daniel Juster, First President of UMJC, Senior Elder-Tikkun International, Prof. Messianic Jewish Studies at The King's University and Messianic Jewish Bible Inst.

Rabbi Kasdan's commentary on the New Testament book of Ephesians clearly argues that Paul, the Christian theologian, is better understood as Sha'ul, the Jewish Rabbi. The book presents a helpful summary of the Messianic Jewish perspectives on Yeshua (Jesus) and Sha'ul (Paul), along with insights into first-century Jewish Christianity.

—Rebecca Moore, Ph.D., Professor Emeritas
Department of Religious Studies
San Diego State University

An excellent resource for individual or small group Bible study! Ephesians was written by a first-century Messianic Jewish rabbi and now we have a commentary on this magnificent epistle written by a modern Messianic Jewish rabbi....an important contribution to the current literature.

—Rabbi David Rudolph, PhD
Director of the Messianic Jewish Studies Program, The King's University

Rabbi Kasdan has done a wonderful job recovering and reconstructing the ancient church's principal theological voice by getting it in conversation with the ancient synagogue's. In this well researched, well written, easy-to-read volume, Rabbi Kasdan helps us discover the man, his message in Ephesians and its meaning for us today—individuals far removed from Ephesus in time and space, but connected to it by faith and grace.

—Dr. Jeffrey L. Seif
Professor of Messianic Jewish Studies, The King's University and Messianic Jewish Bible Institute.

Once again Rabbi Barney Kasdan has made a worthy contribution to the growing body of Messianic Jewish literature, demonstrating the depth of understanding and the maturity of our scholarship. In this work, Rabbi Barney introduces us to the Jewish "misunderstood" Rabbi, Shaul, who addresses the believers in Ephesus. In a clear presentation Rabbi Kasdan exegetes the book of Ephesians' passages from a thoroughly Jewish perspective, taking us back in time and place to the beginnings of the spread of the Jewish Yeshua movement.

—Elliot Klayman
Executive Director, Messianic Jewish Theological Institute

Ephesians—on Walking with Messiah Yeshua is a great resource for anyone seeking a clear understanding of this important letter. By weaving his knowledge of the language, culture, history, and writings of the first century Jewish community together with a clear exposition of Paul's letter, Rabbi Barney Kasdan provides a fresh perspective with invaluable insights. Readers will also find this book written with a simplicity and clarity that makes its message easy to grasp.

—*John Cook, Missions Pastor, Maranatha Chapel and Director, Maranatha Bible College, San Diego, California*

A MESSIANIC COMMENTARY

RABBI PAUL ENLIGHTENS THE

EPHESIANS

ON
WALKING WITH MESSIAH YESHUA

A MESSIANIC COMMENTARY

RABBI PAUL ENLIGHTENS THE

EPHESIANS

ON
WALKING WITH MESSIAH YESHUA

RABBI BARNEY KASDAN

Lederer Books
A division of
Messianic Jewish Publishers
Clarksville, MD 21029

Copyright © 2015 by Barney Kasdan

2   2016

ISBN 978-1-936716-82-1

Library of Congress Control Number: 2015945830

Published by
Lederer Books
A division of
Messianic Jewish Publishers
6120 Day Long Lane
Clarksville, Maryland 21029

Distributed by
Messianic Jewish Resources Int'l.
www.messianicjewish.net
Individual and Trade Order line: 800-410-7647

Email: lederer@messianicjewish.net

Printed in the United States of America

This book is dedicated to some of my early rabbis:
Dr. Charles Feinberg (z"l), Dr. Louis Goldberg (z"l),
Dr. Arnold Fruchtenbaum and Dr. Dan Juster.
Thank you for the "dust" of learning
(Pirke Avot 1:4).

ABOUT THE AUTHOR

Barney Kasdan is rabbi of Kehilat Ariel, a thriving Messianic synagogue located in San Diego, CA. He holds degrees from Biola University (BA History) and Talbot School of Theology (M.Div.). He also completed a year of post-graduate study at American Jewish University in Los Angeles. Rabbi Kasdan is ordained through the Union of Messianic Jewish Congregations and has served on numerous committees including as its President (1998-2002). He has written numerous articles regarding Messianic Judaism and is the author of the popular books *God's Appointed Times, God's Appointed Customs* and *Matthew Presents Yeshua King Messiah* (all by Messianic Jewish Publishers). Among his various duties, he also serves as a Chaplain for the San Diego Police Department. He and his wife Liz reside in San Diego and have four grown children.

CONTENTS

GENERAL EDITOR'S COMMENTS. xi
INTRODUCTION. xv
CHAPTER 1
  Salutation 1:1-2 1
  The Blessing (*Brachah*) 1:3–14 6
  The Provision of Messiah 1:7-12 11
  The Power of the Spirit 1:13-14 15
  The Rabbi's Prayer For Light 1:15-23 17
CHAPTER 2
  The Matchless Grace of God 2:1-10 21
  Gentiles in the Messianic Community 2:11-22 29
CHAPTER 3
  The Mystery of Messiah 3:1-13 47
  The Rabbi's Prayer for Love 3:14-21 54
CHAPTER 4
  Using our Gifts for Messiah's Kingdom 4:1-16 59
  The Pagan Lifestyle or Messianic Renewal 4:17-32 71
CHAPTER 5
  Filled With the Ruach 5:1-20 81
  Messianic Marriage 5:21-33 91
CHAPTER 6
  Messianic Children and Parents 6:1-4 99
  Bosses and Employees 6:5-9 103
  The Spiritual Battle 6:10-18 105
  Personal Notes From The Rabbi 6:19-24 115
CONCLUSION 119
BIBLIOGRAPHY 121
INDEX 125

BOOKS IN THE MESSIANIC COMMENTARY SERIES

PROVERBS
PROVERBIAL WISDOM & COMMON SENSE

MATTHEW PRESENTS YESHUA, KING MESSIAH

RABBI PAUL ENLIGHTENS THE
EPHESIANS
ON WALKING WITH MESSIAH YESHUA

JAMES THE JUST PRESENTS APPLICATIONS OF TORAH

JUDE ON FAITH AND THE
DESTRUCTIVE INFLUENCE OF HERESY

GENERAL EDITOR'S COMMENTS

Nearly all bible commentators emphasize the importance of understanding the historical, cultural and grammatical aspects of any text of scripture. As has been said, "A text without a context is a pretext." In other words, to assume one can understand what God has revealed through those who present his word—prophets, poets, visionaries, apostles— without knowing the context is presumption. To really understand God's word, it's essential to know something about who wrote it and to whom, what was actually said and what it originally meant, when, where, and why it was written.

By now, everyone knows that the New Testament is a thoroughly Jewish book, written nearly entirely by Jews, taking place in and around Israel. The people written about— Paul, Peter, James, John, etc.—were almost all Jews who never abandoned their identities or people. The topics covered—sin, salvation, resurrection, Torah, Sabbath, how to "walk with God," the Millennium, etc.—were all Jewish topics that came from the Hebrew scripture. The expressions used often were Jewish idioms of that day. So, to fully understand the New Testament, it must be viewed through "Jewish eyes," meaning that the Jewish historical, cultural, grammatical must be examined.

There are commentaries for women, for men, for teens, even for children. There are commentaries that focus on financial issues in the bible. Others provide archaeological material. Some commentaries are topical. Others are the works of eminent men and women of God. But, until now, no commentary series has closely looked at the Jewish context of the New Testament books.

In this series, we have invited some of the top Messianic Jewish theologians in the world to contribute their knowledge and understanding. Each has written on a book (or more) of the New Testament they've specialized in, making sure to present the Jewish aspects—the original context—of each book. These works are not meant to be a verse-by-verse exegetical commentary. There are already many excellent ones available. But, these commentaries supplement what others lack, by virtue of the fact they focus on the Jewish aspects.

A number of different authors wrote these commentaries, each in his own style. Just as the Gospels were written by four different men, each with his own perspective and style, these volumes, too, have variations. We didn't want the writers to have to conform too much to any particular style guide, other than our basic one.

You may see some Hebrew expressions or Hebrew transliterations of the names in the New Testament. Thus, one writer might refer to the Apostle to the Gentiles as Paul. Another might write, Shaul, Paul's Hebrew name. Still, another might write Saul, an Anglicized version of Shaul. And some might write Saul/Paul, to reflect, not reject the different ways this servant of Messiah was known.

Another variation is the amount of reference material. Some have ample footnotes or endnotes, while others incorporate references within the text. Some don't have an enormous amount of notes, based on the book they are writing commentary for.

We have plans for a Messianic Jewish commentary series on the entire bible. Although much has been written on the books of the Hebrew Scriptures, and there have been some written by Messianic Jews, there hasn't been a full commentary series on the "Older" Testament. But, we hope to publish such a series in the near future.

So, I invite you to put on your Jewish glasses (if you're not Jewish) and take a look at the New Testament in a way that will truly open up new understanding for you, as you get to know the God of Israel and his Messiah better.

RABBI BARRY RUBIN
Publisher
General Editor

INTRODUCTION

The Jewish Jesus/Yeshua is officially back! After centuries of denial, misinformation and ignorance, there is a growing consensus that Jesus was born a Jew and lived a thoroughly Jewish lifestyle in first century Israel. People have even rediscovered his name (Yeshua) which is pure Hebrew as opposed to the later Greek, Latin or English. As noted in my earlier work (*Matthew Presents Yeshua King Messiah*), both Christians and Jews are acknowledging what should have been obvious. Even Time Magazine predicted in 2008 that one of the top ten trends of modern society would be the "re-Judaizing of Jesus." Recent books in the Jewish community also highlight the emergence of this fresh perspective with such titles as "Kosher Jesus" and "The Jewish Annotated New Testament." This new (renewed) understanding of the historical Yeshua has helped many people to have a deeper appreciation of the Rabbi from Galilee. His life and teachings are now largely seen as being fully rooted in the culture of first century Judaism. Of course it was still a bit controversial with Yeshua's claims of being the Mashiach/Messiah of Israel. But he himself emphatically proclaimed that he was not starting a "new religion" but had come to fulfill messianic promises to Israel and the nations (cf. Matthew 5:17-18). Yet even as this renewed understanding of the Jewish Yeshua takes hold, there is still another religious frontier to be explored.

Saint Paul or Rabbi Sha'ul?

Although many people now understand the Jewish message of Yeshua, many also believe the old perspective on the Apostle Paul. This is especially true in the Jewish community where many of us were brought up with the idea that perhaps "Jesus was a good rabbi" but "Paul converted and started a new religion." Many in the Christian world still accept the teachings of "Saint Paul" as interpreted through the Reformers like Luther and Calvin. While many of the teachings are accurate and a blessing to believers, we must respectfully point out that Paul was not a Roman theologian or from the Renaissance but a Jewish rabbinical student of the first century. If we are to properly understand this writer of most of the New Testament letters, we must also "re-Judaize Paul." This movement to reevaluate the teachings of Paul has started in scholarly circles the last several years. The so-called "new perspective on Paul" has been taking a fresh look on the traditional understanding of his teachings on justification, works and the Law. Such writers as Lutheran scholar Krister Stendahl and theologians E.P. Sanders, James Dunn as well as Anglican scholar N.T. Wright have sought to interpret Paul in closer context to his Jewish culture. Many are now saying that there is in fact a consistency between the differing aspects of the life of Paul.

> "We see Paul the Jew and Paul the apostle of (Messiah), convinced that God's will is that he be both at once,

and therefore never questioning their compatibility, but sometimes having more than a little difficulty reconciling his native convictions with those which he had received by revelation....He desperately sought a formula which would keep God's promises to Israel intact, while insisting on faith in Jesus..." (Sanders, *Paul, the Law, and the Jewish People*, p.199).

While not agreeing with all the recent conclusions of Christian scholars, Jewish academia is also in the process of reevaluating past assumptions about Paul. Jewish biblical scholar Pamela Eisenbaum clearly reflects this trend in the provocative title of her book, *Paul Was Not A Christian*. Her conclusions on Paul are significantly different from ours in the Messianic Jewish world but we do agree with the need to see Paul as a traditional Jew as opposed to the Christian convert presented by the later Church Fathers.

The internal evidence of the New Testament clearly substantiates not only the Jewish Yeshua but also the Jewish Paul. His personal testimony is recorded in several places in the Scriptures. He was born a Jew in Tarsus (modern Turkey) and given the Hebrew name "*Sha'ul.*" Like most Jews who lived outside Israel, he also went by the Greek name "Paul" when he was in the non-Jewish community. In his youth he moved to Jerusalem in order to study at the rabbinical academy of Rabban Gamli'el the Elder who, as the grandson of Hillel, was the top Pharisee teacher of the day (cf. Acts 22:1-3). So respected was this Torah scholar that it is said in the Talmud: "When Rabban Gamli'el the elder died, the glory of the Torah ceased, and purity and saintliness" (Tractate Sotah 9:15). Not

xvii

only was it a great honor to study under this Rabbi but Sha'ul also rose through the ranks to become a leader among his peers. Ironically, it was as he was leading the "Anti-Yeshua Committee", that he had his own personal encounter with the living Messiah (cf. Acts 9).

An interesting note in the Talmud mentions "a certain disciple/*oto talmid*" of Gamli'el who was said to be argumentative with his Rabbi. This unnamed student is described by Gamli'el as an example of those who show "impudence in matters of learning" (Tractate Shabbat 30b). Some scholars believe this would be an apt description of Sha'ul as not only a renegade disciple but also as the strong leader of the early Messianic Jewish movement (cf. Klausner, From Jesus to Paul, p.310).From that point on, this charismatic rabbinical student applied his gifts in furthering the message of Yeshua as the Messiah as he became a *Shaliach*/Apostle for Jews and Gentiles alike.

Besides his auto-biographical information, there are many other proofs of Sha'ul's Jewish background and rabbinic training. Although he is often accused of being anti-Torah, a careful reading of his teaching suggests otherwise. Sha'ul often taught the importance of the Torah/Law and his appreciation for the Torah as that which is "holy, just and good" (cf. Romans 7:12). It is true that he also emphasized how obedience to Torah, no matter how observant, would not suffice for removing our sin. This was accomplished in the beautiful reality of the coming of Messiah Yeshua. Some scholars even misinterpret Sha'ul's perspective on the Torah as he seems to minimize its importance in some cases. But they tend to overlook the fact that he is so often addressing non-Jews who do not have the same Torah obligations as do the Jewish people. A classic case in point is the fact that Sha'ul insisted on his Jewish disciple Timothy being circumcised while he also insisted that his Gentile disciple Titus not be circumcised (cf. Acts 16:1-3; Galatians 2:1-3). Some of these verses are interpreted as if Sha'ul is now a Christian convert and anti-Law. But the teaching of Sha'ul is logically reconciled when one realizes that he is addressing Gentiles in those verses. He never discourages Jews from following their God-given heritage in the written Torah. In fact, he proved his allegiance to the Torah and his Jewish people as he took a Torah vow as a public statement to all (cf. Acts 21:20-24).

In reality, even his teaching of Torah leniency for the Gentiles is very consistent with rabbinic understanding. Non-Jews are not required to keep the 613 commandments but merely the Seven Commandments of the Sons of Noah (Tractate Sanhedrin 56a). Sha'ul agreed with the decision of the Jerusalem Council that these precepts, as summarized by four laws, were all that was required upon Gentiles choosing to follow Yeshua as their Messiah (cf. Acts 15:19-21). When studied carefully in context, the evidence is overwhelming regarding the Jewishness of Sha'ul. He was born a Jew and lived as a Jew, keeping kosher and observing the Jewish holy days (a good article on this truth is found in the essay by Mark Nanos, "Paul and Judaism" in *The Jewish Annotated New Testament*). There are many instances recorded where Paul is observed following Torah and Jewish tradition. He is found attending many synagogue services and even being invited to give the *drash*/message for the day (Acts 13:15). Sha'ul is also found amidst the Jewish holy day celebrations of Passover

(Acts 20:5-6), Shavuot/Pentecost (Acts 20:16) as well as the Fast of Yom Kippur (Acts 27:9). For sure he was a Jew with a controversial message: Yeshua is the risen Messiah for all. But in case anyone would have any doubt of his Jewishness, he was even disciplined several times within the synagogue with the rabbinic mandated 39 lashes (cf. II Corinthians 11:24). Sha'ul was not perceived as starting a new religion but was still considered a Jew by the Jewish authorities of his day. Whatever the perceptions were of Sha'ul in his day or in ours, he makes it clear as to his self-identity when he publicly states (note the present tense), "I am a Jew...I am a Pharisee" (cf. Acts 22:3; 23:6).

A Jewish Understanding of the Letter to the Ephesians

Our interpretations of Sha'ul's letter will be a direct reflection of our interpretation of Sha'ul himself. Was he the Christian theologian Saint Paul or the Jewish Rabbi Sha'ul? At this point, I would like to define a few things about this messianic commentary on Ephesians. In keeping with the Jewish context of the letter, I have used the Complete Jewish Bible (translator Dr. David H. Stern) as the text. This Messianic Jewish translation accurately captures the cultural and religious background of the epistle, as reflected is the use of the name "Sha'ul." The official title to give to Sha'ul is another story. He was certainly an Emissary/*Shaliach*/Apostle and I use these terms freely. Applying the term "Rabbi" to Sha'ul is less clear and understandably debated. Rabbi or Rav (used outside of Israel) means "exalted one" or later "teacher/sage." Many scholars suggest that the office of rabbi was developed in the early first century CE/AD. We find this documented in various sources including the Talmud during the *Tannaim*/early rabbis of the Mishnah (see "Rabbi", Encyclopedia Judaica). Sha'ul's teacher is called Rabban Gamli'el, a title also found with other leaders. The New Testament alludes to several rabbis including some Pharisees (cf. Matthew 23:7-8) and Yeshua himself (cf. *Yochanan*/John 1:38; 3:2; 6:25; 20:16). It also speaks of a spiritual gifting for "teachers" who instruct the messianic body of Yeshua (cf. Ephesians 4:11-12).

Was Sha'ul an ordained rabbi? It is hard to say as the term was just developing in the first century. There is no doubt that Sha'ul was a rabbinical student sitting at the feet of Rabban Gamli'el. Did he receive *s'mikha*/ordination? Did he complete his required studies? Even if he was fully ordained, many things certainly changed as he identified with the Yeshua movement. The historical development of the position of rabbi will continue to be debated but one thing is for sure; we Messianic Jews and Gentiles look to Sha'ul as our teacher and rabbi. In this messianic commentary on Ephesians, I have made the judgment call to use the term "Rabbi" in connection with Sha'ul. I believe the term "Rabbi Sha'ul" gives us 21st century believers a true feel for the original Jewish context of the teacher from Tarsus.

I would also like to define my use of Talmudic passages within this New Testament commentary. By quoting Talmudic and other rabbinic sources, I do not mean to imply that they agree with our philosophy in Messianic Judaism but I am simply illustrating that similar concepts have been discussed by other Jewish sources as well. It is my belief that it is imperative for the rabbinic background to be included in the search to understand the Jewish context of Sha'ul's letters. This, in fact, has often been the missing link in the commentaries on Paul's writings. Professor Shmuel Safrai is among many Jewish scholars who have likewise argued that the rabbinic literature (even that dated well beyond the Second Temple period) must be consulted to understand the context of first century Judaism (cf. Safrai, "The Value of Rabbinic Literature as an Historical Source"). It is logical that if one wants to understand the original context of the New Testament, one must carefully study first century Judaism including the rabbinic literature.

The Purpose of the Letter

After an earlier visit, Sha'ul evidently felt the need to write a follow up letter to these messianic disciples in Ephesus. The new congregation was an interesting mix of Jewish as well as Gentile believers in Yeshua as the Messiah. The first believers were actually Jews from the local synagogue who gladly received Rabbi Sha'ul's message (cf. Acts 19). In a largely non-Jewish city like Ephesus, it was inevitable that many Gentiles would welcome this Good News as well. A major focus of the epistle is elucidating for the Gentile believers how they now come alongside the Messianic Jews in this community of Messiah. It is not surprising, because of these demographics, that the letter spends a great deal of time (chapters 1-3) on the blessings we have through Messiah and what that means to the diverse members. Chapters 4-6 offer much practical wisdom on how to walk as a Yeshua- believer, covering such important areas as life in the messianic synagogue, marriage, family and keys to spiritual victory. The Rabbi naturally makes use of several Jewish illustrations as he teaches these truths such as the Beit Ha-Mikdash/Temple, mikveh for ritual immersion and the Jewish wedding ceremony. All in all, the letter of Ephesians is a wonderful summary (sometimes in Jewish liturgical form) of the good things accomplished through the work of Yeshua as the Mashiach. As stated in Ephesians 1:3: "Praised be Adonai, Father of our Lord Yeshua the Messiah, who in the Messiah has blessed us with every spiritual blessing!" No matter what your background (Jew, Gentile, believer, skeptic), may you also be blessed as you sit at the feet of Rabbi Sha'ul and discover the great riches to be found in Yeshua!

Rabbi Barney Kasdan
May 1, 2015/12 Iyyar, 5775

CHAPTER 1

*"Seven things were created before the world was created:
Torah, repentance, the Garden of Eden, Gehinnom, the
Throne of Glory, the Temple, and the name of the Messiah"*
(Tractate Pesachim 54a)

Salutation 1:1-2

1:1

Sha'ul –

This is the Hebrew name of the writer commonly known
as Paul. He was born to a traditional Jewish family outside
of Israel in the city of Tarsus in Asia Minor (modern Turkey).
As a young rabbinical student, he was invited to study in
Jerusalem with the top Pharisaic Rabbi of the day, *Gam'liel*
(cf. Acts 22:1–3). He must have been a promising and
charismatic leader, as he was on the forefront of opposing the
new Yeshua movement within the Jewish community (cf. Acts
9:1–2). Sha'ul came to personal faith in Yeshua as the Messiah
through a dramatic encounter on a journey to Damascus. From
there, he received his new calling to be a leader in the Yeshua
movement, not only among his own Jewish brothers, but he

1

would especially be instrumental in taking this message of the Messiah to the non-Jewish world of the first century.

As with any Jew of his time (and still today), Sha'ul received two names at birth: a Hebrew name plus a name of the common language of his community. Sha'ul is clearly his given Hebrew name that he would have used in the Jewish community, especially in Israel.

Some commentators believe in Acts 13:9 that Sha'ul took the name Paul (Greek *Paulos*) to prove his "conversion" to a new religion and as a rejection of his previous Jewish life. However, there is every indication that Sha'ul did not look at his messianic faith as a conversion to a new religion, but as a fulfillment of the Jewish hope of the Messiah. In Acts 23:6, Sha'ul proclaims (in the present tense) "I am a Pharisee, a son of Pharisees; I am on trial for the hope and resurrection of the dead." He thus affirmed that he still lived as a traditional Jew even with his new faith perspective. Simply put, Sha'ul was a Jewish follower of Yeshua or, in modern terms, a Messianic Jew. It is important to note that the switch of names in Acts 13 from Sha'ul to Paul is therefore not a statement of conversion but simply reflects the use of his Greek name as he is embarking on his first missionary journey among the Gentiles.

Emissary –

The Greek word used here is *apostolos*, meaning, "One sent out for a particular purpose." In Sha'ul's case, he was designated as one sent out to share the message of Yeshua as the Messiah. However, the foundational Hebrew word, *shaliach*, has a stronger emphasis. A *shaliach* is a person

2

sent out but is also considered "equal to the sender himself" (Tractate Berechot 34). It is an amazing statement of Sha'ul that he considered himself called to directly represent Yeshua himself. Yeshua, having ascended to the Father, delegated his Kingdom work to his hand-chosen apostles (Heb. *sh'lichim*). See Matthew 28:18-20.

Sha'ul was chosen a bit later to help fulfill this messianic mission (cf. I Timothy 2:7). By using this word to describe his calling, Sha'ul is also emphasizing that he speaks the very words that Yeshua had given him. There are those today who believe that the words of Yeshua are truth and that somehow Sha'ul deviated away from his message. Many times people compare the teachings of Yeshua to some apparently contrary teachings of Sha'ul. But these questions are resolved when one remembers the original context of the writers. Yeshua's focus was on the Jewish community of Israel, while Sha'ul's focus was on the Gentile communities abroad. A careful study of both Yeshua and Sha'ul will confirm that they are in complete agreement on the message of the Good News and the broader New Testament. Sha'ul's claim to be an emissary underscores this perspective.

Messiah Yeshua –

Both words are key to a Jewish understanding of Sha'ul's writings. "Yeshua" is the Hebrew personal name for Jesus and means "salvation." This was the original name given to him, as Hebrew names in biblical times were considered descriptive or even prophetic. This one is to be called "Yeshua" because of his mission to his people and ultimately to the entire world (cf. Matthew 1:21).

As the message of Yeshua went international, it is to be expected that the name would be transliterated into various languages. The name Yeshua became Yesus in Greek primarily because the Greek language has no "*shin*/sh" sound but only a "*sigma*/s." Also, European languages often wrote their "y" sound with a "j" that ultimately led in English to the spelling "Jesus." All these transliterations are acceptable, as God is certainly multi-lingual! Yet, while it is acceptable it is preferable that his original Hebrew name be used as a witness to the Jewish people who hear "Yeshua" in synagogue prayers. Also, the name "Jesus" has negative connotations to Jews because of persecution in the name, Jesus.

The second term, "Messiah," is also quite meaningful. The word means "anointed one" and can apply to various individuals in the Scripture, including kings, priests, or prophets. It was understood in Jewish tradition that there would come a unique "Messiah" who would be anointed for the holy mission of world redemption (cf. Daniel 9:24-26; Isaiah 53, the suffering servant, is attributed to the Messiah in Tractate Sanhedrin 98a). Again, the original Hebrew is informative yet underappreciated because of the subsequent translations into different languages.

The original Hebrew, *Mashiach*, or Aramaic, Messiah, was translated by the Greeks as *Christos*. That is why the English word "Christ" often seems foreign and confusing to the average Jew. It seems to speak of a Greek religion or even a foreign god. By using the Anglicized term "Messiah," we are putting the word back closer to the original understanding of all that is implied to the Jewish reader. Undoubtedly, the phrase "Messiah Yeshua" would hold special significance

4

to Sha'ul as a traditional Jew who embraced Yeshua as the promised one.

In Ephesus –

The city was a thriving harbor of Asia Minor (modern Turkey). Being far from Israel, both in distance and in religious lifestyle, Ephesus was primarily a pagan city. It even boasted one of the wonders of the ancient world: the Temple of Diana. While this pagan influence is very observable in the biblical accounts, many forget that the earliest adherents to the Yeshua movement were from the significant Jewish community of the city. We are told that Sha'ul visited the local synagogue for one week as his introduction to the city (Acts 18). Subsequently, he was invited to spend three months in the Jewish community teaching in the synagogue. As a byproduct, the Gentile community was up in arms, as this religious revival was bad for their pagan businesses (Acts 19).

But Sha'ul was encouraged by the open doors at Ephesus and later spent three full years teaching and mentoring these growing Yeshua followers (Acts 20). It is ironic that as Sha'ul makes a pilgrimage to Jerusalem, it is some of the Jewish community of Ephesus who stir up a riot leading to his arrest (Acts 21). It seems to be poetic justice, as Sha'ul, serving out a prison sentence in Rome, writes this letter to the Yeshua followers of Ephesus. Many date this letter at around 60 C.E. (or A.D.), and since the oldest manuscripts do not have the phrase "in Ephesus," many believe that the scroll was actually a circular letter to be read among many messianic communities.

1:2

Shalom –

The word is, of course, a common greeting among Jews, but it is more than that. The root word *shalem* means wholeness, health, well-being, as well as tranquility. Rabbi Sha'ul wishes his readers the peace that can only come from God the Father and Yeshua, the Prince of Peace (cf. Isaiah 9:6).

The Blessing (*Brachah*) 1:3–14

The Plan of the Father 3–6

1:3

"Praised be ADONAI" –

This is another common Jewish phrase seen in such central prayers as the Amidah or the blessing before any meal (*Baruch Atah ADONAI*—Blessed are You, O LORD our God). There is an entire Tractate of the Talmud (rabbinic commentaries on the Scripture) that teaches us the details and importance of saying such blessings (Tractate Berachot). Among the interesting suggestions is that the lover of God should say at least 100 blessings per day in thanks to God, a custom said to have been started by King David (Tractate Menachot 43b; Numbers Raba 18:21).

As Rabbi Sha'ul begins his letter to these followers of Yeshua, it is not surprising that his first thought is to recount some of the *berachot*/blessings that have come from our Father in Heaven. This also explains why verses 3–14 are actually one long sentence in the original language!

ADONAI is a substitute term instead of trying to pronounce the personal name of God. In Hebrew, we have in the Masoretic Text the four letters of God's Name: *Yod-Hey-Vav-Hey* or written in English as YHVH. Since the ancient manuscripts do not give us the vowel sounds, it is only human speculation as to how to pronounce the Holy Name. Jews, being respectful of the Third Commandment, use this term *ADONAI*/LORD as a replacement word. The Talmud explains, "In the Sanctuary the Name was pronounced as written; but beyond its confines a substitute Name was employed" (Tractate Sotah VII.6).

Contrary to what some religious groups say today, no one can say with confidence how to pronounce God's Name. The last book of the New Testament tells us that when Yeshua returns to earth, he will reveal the Name "that no one knew but himself" (cf. Revelation 19:12). It seems best to leave this lost pronunciation unresolved until Messiah comes.

Every spiritual blessing –

God has done so much for his children, yet some seem discontented, as if the Father is holding out on them. Some believers are always looking for a new blessing or experience to validate their faith in Messiah. Sha'ul emphasizes here that we already have every blessing available through the work of Yeshua. True, we may not always be experiencing all those blessings, but the problem is not that God is withholding from us but that we are not fully appropriating those spiritual blessings. Evidently, we do not need more of God, but He needs more of us.

1:4

He chose us –

First among those blessings is the fact that followers of Yeshua have been chosen by God in a special way. Israel's election is a central doctrine of the Hebrew Scriptures (*Tanakh*) as well as present in the Jewish liturgy. From the days of Abraham, God has confirmed that he had a particular calling upon him and his descendants (cf. Genesis 12). The blessing read before chanting the Torah says, *"Who has chosen us from among the peoples."* Sha'ul applies this concept to the Ephesian believers in Yeshua, both Jews and non-Jews. It could be said that for the Messianic Jews of Ephesus they would appreciate the fact that they were in some way "twice chosen." The first time was as a national call to all Israel, but the other time was as one called to be a disciple of Yeshua.

Although these believers of Ephesus in some way responded to God's call, please note that it is God who initiated the covenant call. It is not enough to know the facts of this calling in Messiah. It will only be effectual as each person responds in personal faith to receive that call. This election, unlike Israel's national call, actually took place "before the creation of the universe." Plus, this calling would result in the messianic believers being "holy and without defect." Of course, believers are not perfect and still struggle with sin within our personal lives. That is why Sha'ul does not call us "sinless" but without defect because of our response to this calling. The Good News of Yeshua is that God looks at us, Jew or Gentile, through the work of his Son. He has us covered!

1:5

He determined in advance –

Some translations use the word "predestined" which has led to all sorts of theological debate in both Jewish and Christian circles. Josephus, the first century Jewish historian, notes that this was a debated topic within the various sects of Judaism of his day.

> "As for the Pharisees, they say that certain events are the work of Fate, but not all; as to other events, it depends upon people, themselves, as to whether they take place or not. The sect of the Essenes, however, declares that Fate is mistress of all things and that nothing befalls men unless it is in accordance with her decree. The Sadducees do away with Fate, holding that there is no such thing and that human actions are not achieved in accordance with her decree, but what through personal decisions. Thus, humans are responsible for their own well-being and suffer misfortune through their own thoughtlessness." (cf. Antiquities 13:171-173).

Later Christian theology reflected some of these same discussions. Some extreme views (called the Unconditional View) posited that God makes the determination without any assistance from the person, a concept that seems closely tied to the concept of foreknowledge—that God knew in advance who would believe in Messiah. What is often called the Conditional View of predestination states that because people believe, God then chooses them. This view puts the emphasis on the actions of man as he responds to

God's call. It seems that both sides of this argument have an element of truth in regard to this mysterious working of God. It is not either/or (Unconditional vs. Conditional) but both/and.

God determines certain things in advance, but the freewill of humankind is still essential. If there were no free choice, then it would appear that God is unfair to judge people for their choices. There are too many bible verses stating that "whoever believes" will find this wonderful gift of redemption. As the Torah says, some "secret things belong to *ADONAI*" (cf. Deuteronomy 29:29).

We would be his sons –

Sha'ul points out that one of the dramatic results of Messiah's work is that we, by our personal faith, become sons and daughters of God. In some sense, all humans are children of God by virtue of physical creation and birth. However, not all are related to God in the Spirit realm. Even those born Jewish, who have a covenant with God, must enter into a deeper level of relationship. Yeshua even exhorted a famous rabbi to be "born again" by the Spirit of God (cf. *Yochanan*, or John 3). The phrase here is sometimes translated "adopted" as children. In Jewish law, an adopted child has his original bloodline, but it is his or her legal status that changes. This concept would apply well to both the Jewish and non-Jewish followers of Yeshua in the city of Ephesus. People remained with their cultural identity, but through the work of Messiah, their legal status has changed to become the spiritual children of God.

1:6

Commensurate with the glory of the grace –

All these things lead the writer to give thanks to God for his wonderful grace. The Hebrew word *chen* (grace) means "the unmerited favor of God." Our new relationship with the Father is ultimately not by our own works but is the result of the unearned grace of God as revealed through Yeshua. This idea is emphasized, as Sha'ul uses the same phrase three different times in this opening blessing (v. 6, 12, 14).

The Provision of Messiah 7-12

1:7

We are set free –

The original word evokes the idea of redemption, that is, the purchase of a person for a new relationship. As a Rabbi, Sha'ul seems to be thinking of the ancient Torah ritual of Redemption of the First Born (*Pidyon Ha-Ben*). After the first Passover, all first-born sons of Israel were the priests of their families (cf. Exodus 13:11-15). Later, it was the Levites who were given this holy responsibility by God, and all non-Levite families were instructed to redeem their own first-born son with five shekels (cf. Numbers 18:14-16). As with all the biblical customs given by God, the *Pidyon Ha-Ben* has a higher spiritual meaning. It is actually all mankind that is in need of spiritual redemption. It is only through the blood of Messiah that people are purchased and set free.

Our sins are forgiven –

Judaism teaches the concept of sin using two Hebrew words. One is *chet* meaning, "to miss the target," an apt description of the human condition. People need not be criminals to be "sinners," as the biblical definition means missing the mark and thus falling short of God's standards. All of the Temple sacrifices, especially the *chatat* (sin offering), speak of this need for all people, Israel and all the nations included. One of the key purposes of the work of Messiah is the removal of sin from God's people (cf. Daniel 9:24-25). The New Testament is not proclaiming a new religion, but simply the fulfillment of this messianic promise. No wonder the writer again gives thanks for the wealth of God's grace.

1:9

Made known his secret plan –

The word translated "secret plan" or "mystery" (Gr. *musterion*) is often misunderstood to mean something that cannot be understood. However, the Scriptures use the word to describe the revelation of something not previously known. In this case, the plan of redemption through the coming Messiah, previously predicted in the Hebrew Scriptures *(Tanakh)*, is now fully revealed in the coming of Yeshua.

1:10

Put into effect –

The Greek word *oikonomia* is translated "economy" or "administration." It is used of a structured plan used at a specific time. The English word "dispensation" has been used here and even expanded to include a whole theological perspective on the Scripture. That branch of Christian Systematic Theology says that God works in very specific ways at different set times (e.g. the dispensations of Law and Grace). Another major way of looking at God's "administration" is Covenant Theology. In contrast to differing eras, the thought here is that there is a consistent Covenant spanning all of human history, and that the covenant was first seen in the Torah, which was then superseded by the New Testament.

There are some positive aspects to each of these Christian perspectives but also some weaknesses. It is interesting to note that Judaism has historically not been very concerned with a systematic approach to the Scripture but has tended to take a more holistic view of the entire message. Messianic Judaism may not fall entirely into one of these theologies but also can incorporate elements of both Dispensational and Covenant views. While Sha'ul is not necessarily teaching dispensational theology here, the use of the word emphasizes God's eternal plan now put into effect with the coming of Yeshua. All the covenants and workings of God are in his perfect timing. Nothing is catching the God of the universe by surprise. The entire plan of God is putting everything in creation under the rule of Messiah.

1:11

Given an inheritance –

The Jewish believers of Ephesus could claim a physical inheritance from God, including the Land promised in the *Tanakh* (cf. Exodus 6:8; Deuteronomy 33:4). Messianic

Judaism and many Christian denominations today affirm that God will still fulfill the Land promises to the Jewish people. Something unusual started when the Jewish people returned to the Land of their forefathers with the immigration of the 19th and 20th century. For Messianic Jews, the physical rebirth of the State of Israel is not just about manmade resolutions but is a sign that God still intends to fulfill his Word in a literal way.

While there is a present day controversy over the Jewish State, it should be noted that these land promises do not exclude the modern Arab cousins. There is plenty of land in the Middle East and certainly a way to accommodate the co-existence of both a Jewish state and an Arab Palestinian state if there is a proper recognition of both states. It seems however that the final fulfillment of all the promises will have to wait for the return of Yeshua to Jerusalem.

As Rabbi Sha'ul speaks of the inheritance, it becomes clear that he is also speaking of an inheritance that is focused on spiritual promises. The promise of physical land is not given to non-Jews, but the greater spiritual reality of redemption and relationship with God is. The mixed membership of the Messianic congregation in Ephesus is said to share in a common experience. The Gentile believer does not replace the Jewish believer, but is invited to share the same spiritual promises found in Yeshua and the messianic redemption.

1:12

We who earlier put our hope in Messiah –

This additional phrase emphasizes that the Jewish believer is not joining a new, Gentile religion. This is clear in Sha'ul's mind, because it is the Jewish believers who were the first fruits of this Yeshua movement (cf. Acts 2; Romans 15:8). People may debate the details of God's plan, but the Rabbi emphasizes that this is all by the divine purpose and plan of God the Father. He even repeats the beautiful refrain that this whole spiritual plan brings praise to God commensurate with his glory.

The Power of the Spirit 13-14

1:13

You who heard the message –

See the notes in the Introduction regarding the city of Ephesus and the start of this new messianic community. The Jewish members of the local synagogue, who saw that Sha'ul's teaching was consistent with the Torah, were the foundation of the group. Not only that, the teaching boldly proclaimed that Yeshua brought the way of redemption predicted by the Hebrew Prophets. This was an exciting fulfillment for these Jewish believers, as it is still today for contemporary Messianic Jews. The non-Jews who also heard the message came to understand that the message of the Hebrew Scriptures is inclusive of them (cf. Genesis 12:3; Isaiah 11:1-12). Not all Gentiles believed in the message either, as can be seen by the opposition from many pagans to this Jewish message of redemption (cf. Acts 21). But there was a group of non-Jews, who, along with their Jewish friends, embraced the wonderful message of forgiveness of sin and abundant life only found in Messiah Yeshua.

Sealed by him with the promised Holy Spirit (Ruach HaKodesh) –

The eternal plan of the Father was to be manifested through the provision of Messiah. To this, Rabbi Sha'ul adds an essential ingredient—the power of the Holy Spirit. All these magnificent promises of the Scripture might be for naught if there were no power to implement them. It is here that the Ruach steps in. The reality of the Spirit of God (*Ruach Elohim*) is confirmed many times throughout the *Tanakh* (cf. Genesis 1:2; Isaiah 48:16). It is taught elsewhere that all followers of Yeshua receive this gift of the Spirit when they first come to faith (cf. Romans 8:9; I Corinthians 12:13).

Here the Rabbi uses the analogy of the ancient seal, which closed a document. Such clay or wax seals were used to authenticate the contents of the document and protect them from damage. They were also used to verify the sender, as in the case of the clay seal found in an archaeological dig in the City of David area of Jerusalem. In a burnt room, from the level of the 586 B.C.E. Babylonian destruction, a seal was found engraved with the name *Berechyahu ben Neryahu ha-sofer* (Baruch the son of Neriah the scribe), the precise name of the personal scribe of Jeremiah the Prophet (cf. Jeremiah 36:26).

This ancient custom of sealing documents illustrates what the Ruach (Spirit) has done in the life of every believer in Yeshua. Sha'ul points out to his readers that it is the Ruach of God who is the seal, guaranteeing the validity of the scriptural promises. He is the One who is the down payment of the pledge of messianic redemption. Not only this, the Spirit gives us the necessary power to walk in victory on our current spiritual journey (cf. Acts 1:8). For all this, Sha'ul, now for the third time, gives praise to God with the beautiful blessing (*brachah*), which is a natural response to the glorious works of God.

How about us today? Do we understand the plan of the Father? Can we better appreciate the provision of Messiah? Are we walking in the power of the Ruach that God provided? All these things should lead us to join Sha'ul in giving praise to the Father for his incredible plan of redemption and new life in Yeshua!

The Rabbi's Prayer For Light 1:15-23

1:15

Ever since I heard about your trust in the Lord Yeshua –

Sha'ul pauses at this point of the letter to reflect on some of the amazing blessings from God. This would naturally include the obvious points of the opening paragraph, such as the plan of the Father, the provision of Messiah, and the power of the Ruach. But the *Shaliach* is especially thankful that this group of Jews and Gentiles actually trusted in this great plan and appropriated its riches! The message is the Good News of God, yet that Good News only becomes effective as a person puts his faith in the work of the Redeemer.

1:17

To give you a spirit of wisdom and revelation –

Now that these new believers have started their faith journey with Yeshua, there is a need for increased enlightenment. Wisdom (*Chochmah*) has always been a most treasured possession in Judaism. In fact, true spiritual wisdom can only be found in the

17

fear of *ADONAI* (cf. Proverbs 1:7). Not surprisingly, the entire book of Proverbs (*Mishlei*) s devoted to the acquisition and walk of wisdom. The Rabbi also prays for ongoing revelation (unveiling, Gr. *apokolupsis*) for his disciples, as well. No one comes to Yeshua except by the supernatural process of the Spirit, and no one can truly understand the things of God without the divine revelation of the Father. This is beyond the natural knowledge acquired in the world (Greek, *gnosis*) but is the full knowledge (Gr. *epi-gnosis*) of things of the spiritual realm. It still explains why the message of Yeshua seems so foreign to some while it is the revelation of God to others!

1:18

Light to the eyes of your heart –

Sha'ul uses an interesting metaphor. One would expect to have light for the eyes, but "the eyes of your heart"? It is the Rabbi's way of saying that while most things are observed with the physical eyes, there is another realm of the Ruach not naturally observable. It is within the heart (Heb. Lev) that all the seat of emotions and spiritual life originates. Many prayers in the Jewish prayer book (*siddur*) beseech God to enlighten our eyes to his Torah of truth. It is this same kind of enlightenment that is necessary to truly comprehend the work and words of Yeshua as King Messiah.

1:19

His power working in us –

The emissary also prays that the believers will understand that all this is only by the power of God at work. Here again, we are reminded of the unique approach of Messianic Judaism. It is not only the unique message of the work of Yeshua, unlike any other religious teaching in history, it is the fact that the Spirit now lives within each believer. Like the Ephesians, all followers must depend on a power outside themselves. Blessed be God for the gift of the Holy Spirit (cf. Acts 1:8; I Corinthians 12:13). And most amazingly, this is the very same power that raised Yeshua from the dead and placed him at the Father's right hand!

1:21

Far above any other name –

The Talmud teaches the following: "Seven things were created before the world was created: Torah, repentance, the Garden of Eden, *Gehinnom*, the Throne of Glory, the Temple, and the name of the Messiah" (Tractate Pesachim 54a). In his reflective prayer, Rabbi Sha'ul revels in this truth. It is not just a generic wish for the age to come, but in the name "Yeshua" that the redemptive plan of God can be experienced. In fact, when his name is said, it is a reminder of the "salvation" that God's offers through the Messiah! It is this Yeshua of Nazareth who is thus made head over everything and is the full expression of YHVH, the Holy One, blessed be he!

19

CHAPTER 2

"Rabbi Y'hoshua ben Levi cast together two verses: It is written: 'And, behold, one like a son of man came with the clouds of heaven,' and it is written: 'Humble, and riding on a donkey!' If Israel merits, (Messiah) will come with the clouds of heaven; if Israel does not merit, he will come humble and riding on a donkey'"

(Tractate Sanhedrin 98a).

The Matchless Grace of God 2:1-10

2:1

You used to be dead because of your sins –

Rabbi Sha'ul continues his teaching to these Yeshua followers by discussing the need for the grace of God. As defined above (1:6), the Hebrew word *chen* denotes the unearned favor of the Father. What is this grace? All of the Ephesian believers, both Jews and non-Jews, were once spiritually dead in their sins. What started with the Fall of Adam and *Chava* (Eve) was transmitted through the generations of humanity. Some people object to the idea of "original sin" that developed as a doctrine in Christian theology. Judaism, in contrast, does not emphasize an original sin but that every person is said to be born with two

21

distinct inclinations. One is called the *yetzer ha-tov,* meaning "the good inclination," while the other is called *yetzer ha-ra,* defined as "the evil inclination."

This is illustrated in a creative *Midrash* (rabbinic teaching) of the Talmud, where Rabbi Shimeon points out that the Hebrew word in Genesis 2:7, *vay-yitzer* (and he created) is spelled in a rather unusual way. Instead of a single Hebrew letter, *yod*, there are, in fact, two *yods* that represent the dual *yetzers* (natures) put into mankind (Tractate Berachot 61a). The Jewish emphasis is not so much on a transmitted original sin that plagues humanity, but on a spiritual choice that is before every person. Will we choose the way of self or the way of Torah?

Either by innate character or outward choice, all people sin and fall short of God's plan for life. Like our first forefathers who sinned and thus experienced spiritual death (and ultimately physical death, as well), all people have sinned and experienced both deaths. It is because of the fallen spiritual condition that the grace of God is needed. It is noteworthy that Rabbi Saul does not simply say that they were "slightly challenged" or "minimal sinners." All find themselves in the place of spiritual death and therefore in need of some divine intervention.

2:2

You walked in the ways of the present world (olam hazeh) –

The believers of Ephesus were previously in the state of spiritual death, for they walked according to the values of the present world. This does not mean that this entire present world is terrible or sinful in and of itself. After all, it was God who created and blessed the physical world (cf. Genesis 1). An important Jewish concept is *tikkun olam* (repairing the world). People are indeed here in this present age for the holy purpose of bringing the light of God and Torah values to those around them. *Olam hazeh* is also comparable to the Greek idea of *"cosmos,"* meaning the skewed values and priorities of those who do not know God. Yeshua summarized it well when he noted that his followers would be "in the world but not of the world" (cf. John 17:15-16). The Ephesian community walked in the way of the *olam hazeh*.

The Ruler of the Powers of the Air –

While the God of Israel is the Sovereign King, there is also a spiritual battle taking place as a consequence of the fall of mankind. Many reject the idea of a Devil or Satan in modern society, but the evidence of his existence is seen every day in humanity. Put it this way: if there is no Satan, then someone seems to be doing a great imitation of him.

The concept of Satan is not a later Christian invention. Rather, it is imbedded in the theology of Judaism itself. It was Satan who pleaded with God to test Job (cf. Job 1-2). Similarly, it was Satan who accused the High Priest, Joshua, of spiritual decay (cf. Zechariah 3). A reminder of the reality of Satan in Jewish theology is the fact that the name "Satan" actually comes from Hebrew, meaning "one who opposes" or "adversary."

Satan is said to be one of the fallen angels who led a rebellion even before the creation of the world (cf. Isaiah 14; Ezekiel 28). The rabbis of the Talmud speak many times of Satan and his evil influence in God's world. It is pointed out

23

that his title (*Ha-Satan*) has the numerical value in Hebrew of 364. Because of this, Satan has the power to accuse Israel 364 days a year, but he has no power on the holiest day of the Jewish year, *Yom Kippur*/Day of Atonement (Tractate Yoma 20a). In Jewish thought, the principal antidote for the accusations of Satan is the study of Torah (Leviticus Rabbah 28.3). Yeshua himself had his direct confrontation with the Adversary, and, in good Jewish fashion, he used the Torah to fight his way to victory as he quoted verses from Deuteronomy (cf. Matthew 4:1-11). What an important example that is to modern followers of Yeshua! On the basis of all this, it is quite understandable that Rabbi Sha'ul notes that it is this evil presence of Satan that plagued the Ephesian believers in their past manner of life.

2:3

In our natural condition, we were headed for God's wrath –

The challenge of all humanity is to make the right choices in regard to the things of God. The "evil inclination" (*yetzer ha-ra*) constantly beckons us to follow our own way. The natural way of mankind leads to the neglect of God, the Torah, and ultimately to the judgment of God. The condition of all humankind, like the Ephesian believers, is so needy that it requires outside help. Those who believe that they can please God with their own efforts need only keep a ledger of how many times they fall short and disappoint the Father in Heaven. It would be a sad message if this were the last verse of the letter.

2:4

But God is so rich in mercy –

The Good News of the *Tanakh* and the New Covenant is that, while we fall short, God has provided a gracious way of reconciliation through the Mashiach. This mercy and grace of the Father is seen in the fact that, while we were dead in our disobedience, he sent Yeshua for the restoration of all those who embrace his name. As defined above (1:6) the *chen* (grace) of God bestows on others blessings that are undeserved. Sha'ul also uses the term *rachem* (mercy), which emphasizes the opposite side of this truth. While grace is receiving some undeserved blessings, mercy is the withholding of the judgment that is rightly deserved. Both concepts are beautiful pictures of God's intense love for his world and reminders of his deliverance for all those who receive his gift of Yeshua.

2:6

God raised us up with the Messiah Yeshua –

Part of the evidence of God's mercy is the victory over death. This is undoubtedly one of the unique aspects of the message of the *Tanakh* as well as the New Covenant. Many religions and philosophies have exalted teachers and leaders. The Jewish Scriptures, however, promise something even greater, victory over the greatest enemy of mankind —death. Part of the promise of the coming Mashiach is that he would conquer this last challenge. Numerous Scriptures in the *Tanakh* foretell this great victory over physical death and the coming resurrection (cf. Isaiah 26:19; 53:10-12; Daniel 12:1-2).

Rabbinic theology found itself somewhat puzzled in regard to the predicted death of Mashiach. Clearly there are many Scriptures, which speak of the Messiah "being cut off from the living" in some sort of premature death (cf. Isaiah 53:8; Daniel 9:26; Zechariah 12:10). Yet there are even more verses which speak of the Messiah ruling as the King of Israel (cf. Genesis 49:10; Isaiah 9:6; Micah 5:2). How could these two vastly different descriptions of the Mashiach be reconciled? One interpretation posits that there may be in fact two different Messiahs coming for these two different missions. Mashiach ben Yosef (Messiah son of Joseph) will be the one to suffer, like Joseph of Genesis, and ultimately be killed. He will be followed by Mashiach ben David (Messiah son of David) who will come to rule as King, like his forefather David (Tractate Sukkah 52a).

Is it two Messiahs for the two missions or one Messiah who appears twice? The New Testament agrees with the two-fold mission of the Messiah, but offers a unique explanation. Rabbi Sha'ul makes it clear where he stands on this question. Yeshua died on a Roman cross to fulfill the first mission of Mashiach. The testimony of the New Covenant is that this "Yeshua of Nazareth" is confirmed to be the Promised One because God raised him from the dead as the first fruits of the resurrection (cf. Romans 1:1-4). But the mercy of God does not stop there! Rabbi Sha'ul points out that God has also raised up all followers of Yeshua to a new reality. We indeed have the hope of the future resurrection in *Olam HaBa* (the World to Come), but God has also raised us up to a new heavenly reality of being spiritually born again. This must be one of the greatest proofs of God's marvelous mercy and kindness shown to those who receive the gift of Yeshua's redemption. It also explains why Messianic Jews and Christians look for the return of the risen Yeshua to fulfill the second part of his mission, to rule as King over Israel and the World.

2:8

Delivered by grace through trusting –

This great salvation and deliverance is not a result of our own religiosity or even *mitzvot* (good works). Sha'ul emphasized that it is ultimately an unmerited free gift of God by *chen* (grace). Some would say that the salvation of God is an unconditional promise to all, but the Rabbi gives one important condition of experiencing this grace. It is essential that a person, Jew or non-Jew, display a personal faith by trusting in the work of Messiah. This is precisely where so many people are confused or deceived. It is not enough to know the message of the Scripture or even to be a consistent member of a synagogue or church. The key question to ask ourselves is if we have personal, living faith in that message, and apply that faith by trusting in Yeshua. Ultimately, we are merely receiving the great gift that God has offered us. The grammar of the verse is sometimes debated.

What is it that is not our own accomplishment? Is it our trusting faith in Yeshua, as some conjecture? This interpretation leads to the conclusion that since even our faith is a gift from God then we essentially have no real part in our redemption. However it should be noted that the pronoun "this" would need to agree with the feminine form for the word "trusting." Yet, the pronoun is in the neuter grammatical form, thus agreeing with the word "delivered." Sha'ul points out the logical conclusion that if all this is by God's grace, then we have no opportunity for pride in ourselves. There is no boasting in ourselves but only in what God has done for us through Yeshua. Here again we see a stark contrast to other religions and philosophies that are based on man's religious effort. In the world we can often witness "religious" individuals who then take pride in their own efforts. The message of the Scriptures takes away the temptation for religious pride as we realize our need and Messiah's provision.

2:10

A life of good actions –

As we realize the unique grace of God and his way of redemption, this is not to say that we ignore the importance of *mitzvot* (good deeds). Some might take the teaching of God's grace to the false conclusion that we cannot do anything worthy in our daily life. Indeed it is an important Jewish value to be a blessing through *tikkun olam* (repairing the world). This is good and commendable, but it is not the whole story of this Scripture. Some today act as if their whole salvation is simply dependent upon the amount of good works they perform. Rabbi Sha'ul provides a perfect biblical balance to both ends of the spectrum of spiritual faith versus good works. The Scripture paints it this way: our works are not the basis of our salvation, but they are indeed the residual fruit that we already have this salvation.

Some people, even theologians, misinterpret Sha'ul's teachings to think that he emphasizes personal faith alone to the exclusion of good works. Perhaps this has been a response to the overemphasis on the importance of good deeds. In his letter to the Ephesians, Rabbi Sha'ul gives his perspective that both aspects are vital in their own way. How ironic it is that he addresses the importance of both trusting and good actions in these two connected verses! Messianic Judaism greatly appreciates the free gift of God in bringing us salvation through Yeshua. This does not negate the priority of the *mitzvot* (good works), but gives us an even deeper motivation to let our works shine in the world around us. Mashiach has brought light into our lives, so now we can let that light shine as a testimony of his presence in our lives (cf. Matthew 5:14-16). Do people notice the presence of Yeshua in our daily lives? Are we fulfilling our call to do *mitzvot* as a testimony of our new life in him?

Gentiles in the Messianic Community 2:11-22

2:11

Remember your former state, you Gentiles by birth –

Up to this point of his letter, Rabbi Sha'ul has been addressing the common experience of all the believers of Ephesus through their similar faith in Messiah. He now turns his attention to the non-Jewish believers of Ephesus and some unique aspects of their spiritual journey to Yeshua. The word "Gentiles" is not a negative or pejorative term; it simply reflects the translation from the Hebrew word *goyim* (Greek *ethne*), meaning "nations." *Am* is the word usually associated with the Jewish people while "*goyim*" is related to all other

29

people. While God has made a special covenant with Israel, he has also shown equal love for all the people of his creation. Yet, because of the unique covenant with the descendants of Abraham, Isaac, and Jacob, it was clear that the non-Jewish people did not have a direct covenant relationship with God (cf. Genesis 12:1-3). Sha'ul's point is that this all changed with the coming of the Messiah, Yeshua, who is the manifestation of God's grace to all people, Jews and Gentiles alike. He starts this paragraph with the word "therefore," focusing attention on the previous concept of God's *chen* (grace). There are some dramatic new realities applied to the Gentiles who have responded to God's grace as manifested in Yeshua as Messiah and Lord.

Called the Uncircumcised –

While the Scripture does not speak in negative terms about the Gentiles or nations, it undoubtedly could become a reference to the pagan background of those not born Jewish. Only the Jewish nation followed the eighth day *Brit Milah* (Circumcision) as a sign of the Abrahamic Covenant (cf. Genesis 17). It is easy to understand how the term "uncircumcision" was not only a statement of physical appearance but also of the state of their spiritual life. As circumcision is the removal of the flesh, so too there is a circumcision of the heart where one's spirit is pure before God (cf. Deuteronomy 30:6). It would be tempting for Jews in covenant relationship with God to refer to the pagan non-Jews in the world as the "uncircumcised" in reference to both their physical and spiritual life.

2:12

At that time had no Messiah –

By definition, a first-century Gentile would in fact be a pagan. This was easily observable in the day-to-day life of such a diverse city as ancient Ephesus. While there was a significant Jewish presence and a synagogue community in the city, it was a distinct minority within the Roman, or pagan, majority. In contrast to the strict monotheism of Judaism, the non-Jewish community of Ephesus would have prided itself on its many gods and religious pluralism. Almost any religious doctrine could be found in this pagan society except for the unique teaching of Judaism as found in the Messianic doctrine. The idea of a single king ruling a utopia of the one true God would have seemed absurd and unnecessary to the average Gentile in that day. In the previous life of the Ephesian Gentiles, they were unaware of the teaching of a coming Messiah and the need for his redemption. It should be noted that there certainly was a group of non-Jews who were hearing the message of the Scriptures. It is well documented in history that there were many *yireh ha-shamayim* (God-fearers) who attended the local synagogues. This was a large group disenchanted with the pagan society and subsequently drawn to the monotheism and ethics of Judaism. It is logical that many of the early Gentile believers in Yeshua (including from Ephesus) identified as God-fearers, and thus were prime candidates for the message of the messianic hope as well.

Estranged from the national life of Israel –

Similarly, before their awareness of the messianic redemption, the non-Jews of Ephesus were estranged from

31

the Jewish people and Judaism in general. The Greek word translated "national life" is "*politeia,*" meaning citizenship, way of life, or commonwealth. By their pagan culture and religion, they were estranged from the revelation of the true God given to Israel. It is an apt description as the Gentiles were not in proper relationship with the true God, nor with his people. Sha'ul will soon describe the change in status for these followers of Yeshua. The Gentiles who had come to true faith in Yeshua have not become Jews or even spiritual Jews. Sha'ul is careful to make that clear, yet also affirming that the non-Jewish believers in Yeshua were now affiliated with Israel in a special way.

Perhaps the word "commonwealth" best captures the new relationship. For example, at different times of history, Great Britain has had many satellite countries as part of its Commonwealth. They are distinct both culturally and ethnically yet they are connected to the larger British Commonwealth. It is an apt picture of all Gentile believers in the Messiah in this present age. No matter what cultural or ethnic distinction, the non-Jewish messianic believer or church-attending Christian is now connected to the Jewish people. They do not replace Israel but, as the Rabbi says elsewhere, they become partakers of the spiritual blessings with the Jewish believers and uniquely connected to the olive tree of Israel (cf. Romans 11:17-18).

Unfortuntely, this truth has not always been embraced by the historic church. Starting with the early church fathers (and continuing through many ages), theologians cut off any connection between Christians and Jews. The estrangement has been devastating for both the church and the synagogue. The term "Christian anti-Semitism" should have been an oxymoron, but was manifested largely because of ignorance of the New Testament teaching. It is a blessing to see in our day a fresh understanding and appreciation by many Christians as to their connection to the Jewish people and Israel through their faith in the Jewish Yeshua. This renewed understanding (much of it based on Sha'ul's teaching) can only serve to be a source of healing between the church and synagogue in these days.

Foreigners to the covenants –

Sha'ul continues to describe the predicament of the pagans. Obviously they were foreigners to the spiritual covenants that God made with the Jewish people and the earlier chosen line (cf. Adam, Noah, Abraham, and Moses). But it seems that the Rabbi is referring to more than just the fact that they were strangers to those agreements. He seems to use a technical term describing the three different categories of non-Jews as understood within Jewish theology.

The Greek word *xenos* used here is directly parallel to the Jewish concept of *nochri* (stranger or foreigner). This refers to a Gentile who happened to be visiting Israel but remained within his own people and culture. Such a person would be of course respected as an individual but would have no automatic rights within the Jewish culture, nor would he even be interested in connecting to the Jewish people.

A second category was called *yireh ha-shamayim* (fearer of heaven). This God-fearer took things a step further as a non-Jew living within the Jewish community. Unlike the *nochri* who essentially stayed to himself, the God-fearer desired to connect in some ways to Judaism and the Jewish

33

people. Many were attracted to the monotheism of Judaism or perhaps the moral values that stood in stark contrast to their pagan society. This person was called by this name because they had a new fear and respect for the true God, the God of Israel. As such, they would become more involved in the life of Israel and even attend the local synagogue services in order to grow in their spiritual understanding. One distinction would be made however. With all their involvement in the Jewish community, the God-fearer stopped short of fully converting to the Jewish faith.

The third category of non-Jew in the first century was called a *ger* (alien). This person would follow the path of the God-fearer with his involvement and interest in the Jewish faith, but he would take it further. Consistent with the teaching of the Talmud, this person could be called a *ger* (convert) if he followed three essential requirements: undergo the rite of circumcision, bring a sacrifice to the Temple and have a ritual immersion (*mikveh*) in water to testify of their serious commitment (Tractate Yevamot 47a). The ger was not just an attendee of synagogue, but one who fully embraced the Torah. To add to the diversity, it was also recognized that even the *ger* could have different levels of identity. A *ger toshav* (sojourning convert) was one who had not adopted Judaism in its entirety but merely the seven laws given to Noah. It was the *ger tzedek* (sincere convert) who fully accepted Judaism out of inner conviction. It is noteworthy that the Jerusalem Council, when faced with the question of the early non-Jews who embraced Yeshua as their Messiah, decided that the model of the *ger toshav* would best fit this growing community (cf. Acts 15).

These three types of non-Jewish individuals appear at various times of Israel's experience (Ruth, Cornelius, etc.). It is the first type (*nochri*), which Sha'ul applies to the Ephesian Gentile believers before they came to faith. They were totally disconnected from God and the covenants as they were evidently entrenched in their own pagan world.

Without hope and without God –

This is Rabbi Sha'ul's logical conclusion in regard to the past life of the non-Jews of Ephesus. The pagan religions and philosophies offered some short-term explanations of life in this present world. There were gods for almost every facet of their life but there were some unresolved dilemmas, the greatest being to have hope beyond death. It is only in the life and work of Yeshua as the Messiah that there is an assurance of hope beyond this life.

The Rabbi also makes the bold statement that, because of their non-biblical beliefs, they were in fact without any real connection to the true God of Israel. It is noteworthy that the Roman and Greek philosophies offered plenty in the way of religion, but without the redemption and mediation of the Mashiach, there remained a separation between them and God.

This message of the Bible remains true in our day even despite the pluralistic influences found in our contemporary culture. The life and work of Yeshua makes him stand apart from all other religious teachers. There is no other religious teacher who claimed to die as an atonement for sins. Ultimately there is no long-lasting hope or even close relationship with the true God without the High Priest, Yeshua (cf. John 14:6).

2:13

But now…you have been brought near –

The non-Jewish followers of Yeshua from Ephesus had now experienced a change of religious status. Although they were previously lost in the pagan world and values, they were now brought close to the true God. The Rabbi points out that this was implemented by the shedding of Messiah's blood on their behalf. The language evokes the system of the Jewish Temple in Jerusalem where there were daily animal sacrifices to atone for the sins of Israel. Of course the Temple system was all a picture of the reality that God would someday fulfill by sending the Messiah. What the *korbanot* (sacrifices) could only temporarily cover, the sacrifice of the Mashiach would make a permanent atonement as his own blood was shed (cf. Daniel 9:24; Isaiah 53:10).

It is important to note that, unlike rabbinic Judaism, there is no need for the Gentile believer to convert to Judaism. There have always been a remnant of non-Jews who choose to identify with Israel and the Jewish people but there are no biblical details of how this happened. The classic example is Ruth who simply makes the choice to stand with her Jewish in-laws when she says, "Your people will be my people, and your God will be my God" (cf. Ruth 1:16). There is no mention of her taking any conversion classes and she is never called a "Jew," but rather Ruth the Moabitess (cf. Ruth 4:10).

It is understandable that there have been non-Jews who desired to strongly identify with the Jewish people. Some are intermarried to a Jew and some just have a Jewish heart. The desire to identify is commendable but the theological reality is that there is absolutely no need for a Gentile conversion to Judaism, including to Messianic Judaism. Though the various denominations of rabbinic Judaism offer such a conversion, I believe that Messianic Judaism shows its uniqueness in that Gentiles are completely welcomed to the Yeshua faith as Gentiles. Rabbi Sha'ul even says it more strongly in another letter:

> Only let each person live the life the Lord has assigned him and live it in the condition he was in when God called him. Was someone already circumcised when he was called? Then he should not try to remove the marks of his circumcision. Was someone uncircumcised when he was called? He shouldn't undergo *b'rit milah* (cf. I Corinthians 7:17-18).

The amazing power of the Good News of Yeshua is that Jews do not need to convert to become Gentiles and the Gentiles who embrace Yeshua have been brought near to God without any conversion. This is certainly one of the main reasons that the Yeshua movement appealed to the seeking Gentile world!

2:14

He himself is our shalom –

The work of Yeshua has brought peace between us and our Father in Heaven. One of the sacrifices of the Torah is called the *sh'le-mim* offering. Based on the word *shalem*, it symbolizes the reality that the person has peace with God that results in peace with those around him (cf. Leviticus 3). How true it is that Yeshua has brought that ultimate peace with God and provided a new positive attitude with the people in our lives. Although Sha'ul is primarily addressing the Gentile readers of his letter, he also includes the Jewish believers with the use of the word "our." There are surely some cultural differences between many types of followers of Yeshua, but we all stand before God in an equal manner. Yeshua, the Prince of Peace, brings shalom equally to both Jew and Gentile alike in this messianic faith.

He has made us both one –

The Jewish believers of Ephesus had a vastly different culture and upbringing than the Gentile majority of the city. They started on very diverse paths but, through Yeshua, they had come to the same conclusion. Sha'ul is not confusing cultural identities here. The Jewish believers did not need to become "Gentilized" nor did the Gentile believe need to become "Judaized." Yet they both were made one and united in this international faith of Yeshua.

Still today there are those who insist that Messianic Jews "convert" to become "Gentile Christians." This is just plain wrong and ironic since it is the Gentiles who have actually become part of the commonwealth of Israel! It is to the glory of God that Jewish believers continue to love their heritage and live Jewish lives. This is why the idea of a "messianic synagogue" has reappeared in our day as a practical way for Jewish believers in Yeshua to live a Jewish lifestyle. If you are Jewish, you should prayerfully consider that it is our calling, "for his free gifts and his calling are irrevocable" (cf. Romans 11:29).

Similarly, the freedom of the Gospel does not require the Gentile believer to become Jewish. Some people expect other believers to look and behave like their church or synagogue. Some even get upset at the fact that there are so many denominations for the New Testament believers. Instead of seeing it as a negative factor, Rabbi Sha'ul sees the diversity within the Body of Yeshua as praiseworthy. The Messianic faith can encompass every tribe, tongue and people. Sha'ul is not calling for uniformity but a unity that embraces diversity. Those who become exclusive or divisive miss a key point of the Good News. There is a wonderful oneness among all those who truly follow Yeshua as Messiah.

Broken down the *m'chitzah* which divided us –

The Rabbi illustrates the previous point with a cultural phenomenon that was quite obvious in his day. *M'chitzah* is the dividing wall which was the norm in both the *Beit Ha-mikdash* (Temple) as well as in virtually every synagogue of antiquity. The Jerusalem Temple was still standing at the time of this letter until its destruction by the Romans in 70 C.E.

The several courtyards of the Temple were divided in order to accommodate different groups of people coming to worship. The Court of the Levites was the inner area exclusively for the priests and their holy service. The next outward court was called the Court of Israel, accessible by any Jewish male. The Court of the Women followed this. Jewish women who had come to pray and worship could only travel this far. The outer area was known as the Court of the Gentiles, which was set aside for any non-Jewish visitors or worshippers like the God-fearers (2:11). Gentiles could not proceed beyond the dividing wall beyond their own courtyard. This was confirmed in recent years with an archaeological find near the Temple Mount in

Jerusalem. Amid the piles of ancient stones, one large stone was engraved in Greek with the following: "No man of another nation shall enter within the fence and enclosure round the Temple. And whoever is caught will have himself to blame that his death ensues!"

The Jewish/Roman historian Josephus describes how this warning was placed in a prominent place at the dividing wall between the Court of the Gentiles and the Court of the Women (Jos. War 5, V, 2). It was standard procedure for there to be various areas of separation in the local synagogues as well. Jewish men and women normally did not sit together but were separated by a balcony or divided area. To this day in most Orthodox *shuls* (synagogues) there are *m'chitzhah*s that are partitions or barriers separating the men and the women.

With this historical background one can appreciate the radical statement of Rabbi Sha'ul regarding Gentile believers. The wall of division has been broken down by the work of Yeshua! In the spiritual sense, Jew and Gentile stand equally before God and can worship together in spirit and in truth. It is curious that many times in history it was assumed that with the broken down wall that it was the Jews who could run over to the Gentile side. Sha'ul's analogy, however, teaches the opposite! It is the Gentile follower of Yeshua who is now welcome to come over to the Jewish side. They need not become Jews (as discussed above) but it would seem that they would have a great appreciation for the fact that they were now welcome to draw close to God through the Messiah. This fact was largely ignored or misapplied in Church history. But we are living in a day when more and more Gentile Christians are appreciating their spiritual Jewish heritage and are thanking God that the wall of partition has come down in Yeshua!

2:15

By destroying the enmity occasioned by the Torah –

Unfortunately, this verse is interpreted by many to mean that the Torah itself causes the enmity or is the problem. It is true that Jews who keep the Torah would by necessity be divided from the Gentiles. For example, a kosher Jew cannot eat a meal at the home of a non-Jew, at least in the view of rabbinic interpretation. While some of this is true, it cannot be the full understanding of this verse. It actually leads some Christian theologies to assert that the Torah is now annulled so Gentiles can fellowship with Jews. But this is contrary to the teaching of Yeshua himself who upheld the Torah and claimed that he did not come to abolish even one letter of the Torah (cf. Matthew 5:17-18). Consequently, it is more logical to interpret that it is not the Torah which is done away by the work of Yeshua, but the enmity between Jew and Gentile, which is abolished.

The wall of partition is derived from a man-made idea, one that is not given in the Scriptures. One of the core values of Messianic Judaism is that the Torah is the eternal word of God and should be respected as such. The problem is not with the Torah but with how some people misinterpret or misapply the holy Torah. When examined, it becomes clear that Sha'ul never denigrated the Torah but was concerned about those who misapplied it. As he said elsewhere: "We know that the Torah is good, provided one uses it in the way the Torah itself intends" (cf. I Timothy 1:3-11).

The simple message of the Gospel is that Jews and Gentiles can live in their respective cultures and be unified by a common faith in the one Messiah. This is the "single, new humanity" that Rabbi Sha'ul discusses. Yeshua has made all, Jew and Gentile, united as one by killing the enmity between both groups through his execution on a criminal's cross. That unity was a powerful testimony of the power of God's message in the first century.

What a blessing to see the unity today between many different kinds of believers: Messianic Jews and Christians alike. It seems to fulfill the popular Jewish expression from Psalm 133: *Hiney mah tov u-mah naim, shevet achim gam yachad* (Behold how good and pleasant it is for brothers to dwell together in unity).

2:17

Shalom to you far off and nearby –

Messiah's atoning work and resurrection have resulted in true shalom for both Gentiles (far away from God) and Jews who follow Yeshua (those nearby). The Rabbi brings out a direct quote of the truth predicted by the prophets that this would be one of the results of the Good News coming from God (cf. Isaiah 57:19)— access to God by this way of salvation.

The Talmud makes use of this phrasing as well in the following quote: "An idol appears to be near at hand but is in reality far off...On the other hand, the Holy One, blessed be He, appears to be far off, but in reality there is nothing closer than He" (Tractate Berachot 13a). Rabbi Sha'ul's wording is very informative as it encompasses all three aspects of God's revelation—access to the Father, through the Messiah in the power of the *Ruach* (Spirit).

2:19

No longer foreigners and strangers –

Having described the strained relationship between pagan Gentiles and the God of Israel, Rabbi Sha'ul exults in the fact that their spiritual status has changed. The Gentile believer in Yeshua is no longer a foreigner (2:11) but now has been brought into the family of God. They are in fact now fellow-citizens with the Jewish remnant with equal standing before God.

2:20

Built on the foundation of the emissaries –

Because this new community of Jews and Gentiles is united in the Messianic faith, they are also equipped for a new purpose. God predicted long ago that there would someday be a spiritual temple that would encompass all of his redeemed children (cf. Amos 9:11-12). Here Sha'ul describes that temple starting with the foundation that consists of the emissaries, *sh'lichim* (Heb.) apostles (Greek).

While a *shaliach* may be a more generic term, meaning one sent out on a mission, no doubt Sha'ul is thinking of the founding twelve *sh'lichim* who have a unique place in history. These were the twelve chosen by Yeshua who walked with him for his 3½ year ministry in Israel. It is these original apostles who received the divine word of God through Yeshua and in fact served as a direct representative of Messiah (1:1). This new temple is founded upon the Jewish disciples who were eyewitnesses to the life and message of Yeshua as King Messiah. That is another reason why every Christian should have a natural love and appreciation for Israel and the Jewish people. Their faith is built upon this Jewish foundation.

And the prophets –

Along with the foundational emissaries, Rabbi Sha'ul notes also the importance of the prophets. This is a reference to the *Neviim*, the Prophets, of the Hebrew Scriptures, read in the synagogue every Shabbat. Traditional Judaism has always affirmed the divine inspiration of these messengers from God. Their words are understood as the progressive revelation of the Word of God

It is quite natural, therefore, to see Sha'ul's reference to the importance of the Jewish prophets in regards to the revelation of the Messiah. This would include the numerous predictions of the coming Messiah and how to recognize him. Such amazing details as the Messiah's lineage (Genesis 49:10), his place of birth (Micah 5:2), as well as his death and resurrection (Isaiah 53) and many more facts predicted by the Prophets are persuasive about his Messiahship.

2:21

In union with him –

Through this new Messianic faith, Jews and non-Jews are united with him for a new divine purpose, not just building a temple for God but the temple itself! The Spirit now dwells in all Yeshua-believers and thus we become that dwelling place of God's presence. This meant a lot to the believers of the first century as they contemplated the Temple in Jerusalem, still standing. How much more significant to modern followers of Yeshua since there has been no Temple standing for nearly 2000 years! Yet the very presence of God now lives in the hearts of his true followers. All believers – Jews, Gentiles, men, women, slave and free—have equal access to God and a dynamic unity among themselves through the work of Messiah.

CHAPTER 3

"The Holy One, blessed be He, looks to the peoples of the world, hoping that they will repent and so bring them near beneath His wings"

(Numbers Raba 10.1).

The Mystery of Messiah 3:1-13

3:1

Prisoner of the Messiah Yeshua –

As was previously noted, Sha'ul is writing this epistle as he is incarcerated in a Roman prison (1:1). It is not the only such letter as it is clear that there were several written that became known as the Prison Epistles. Those mentioned specifically are Philippians, Colossians and Philemon. It is interesting that the Rabbi does not state here that he is a prisoner of Rome or some injustice of a pagan system. He sees God's purpose even in his time in jail, not unlike Joseph did in Genesis when Pharaoh locked him up. In this case, Sha'ul is convinced that he is a prisoner of Yeshua because of the message and for the sake of the Messiah. Much of this letter of Ephesians can be even more greatly appreciated as one keeps in mind that these are not pious religious platitudes from a rabbi living in comfort. It is clear that Sha'ul strongly believes all that he is teaching in spite of (or maybe as a result of!) his own troubles.

On behalf of you Gentiles –

From the earliest verses of the Torah the message of blessing, given first to the Jews, would also extend to all the nations (cf. Genesis 12:1-3). The Prophets of Israel continued to confirm that the Gentiles would also receive many blessings from God because of the Mashiach (cf. Isaiah 11:1-10; Amos 9:11-12). The Talmud likewise understood that God would ultimately reach out to the Gentiles as well: "The Holy One, blessed be He, looks to the peoples of the world, hoping that they will repent and so bring them near beneath His wings" (Numbers Raba 10.1). Sha'ul understood the clear call of God on his life as a *shaliach*/ emissary to the Gentiles (cf. Romans 11:13-14).

With this calling came a tremendous amount of risk as he travelled to distant lands and proclaimed a controversial message, both within the Jewish community and also the Gentile community, although for different reasons. While Jews needed to deal with the messianic claims of Yeshua, the Gentiles also had to deal with the rebuke of paganism and rampant immorality in their ranks. Still Sha'ul persisted and boldly brought this message of hope throughout the Roman Empire at great risk to his personal safety. How ironic it was to see a traditional Jewish rabbi under arrest for his loving ministry to those outside his own people, Israel! This is a reminder to all Gentile believers that they owe a debt of gratitude to the early Jewish believers who brought the message of Yeshua to them (cf. Rom. 15:27).

3:3

This secret plan was made known –

The secret plan of God (Gr. *musterion*) has been discussed before by Sha'ul (1:9). The word does not imply something that cannot be known, but rather an unseen reality that has now been revealed. He uses an interesting phrase to describe the revelation of this truth —the word *apokalupto* (revealing or unveiling). This concept is reminiscent of part of the Jewish wedding ceremony.

A distinctive element of the ceremony is the veiling of the bride by the groom just before the actual ceremony. This dates back to the problematic wedding of our forefather Jacob where he did not check carefully under the veil of his bride and ended up with the surprise marriage to Leah (cf. Genesis 29). Since that time, Jewish grooms make sure to veil their bride just before the ceremony to confirm they have the right one! During the ceremony the veil is lifted to reveal the identity of the bride as they start their new relationship together as husband and wife. This truth would seem to apply to the "mystery" to which Sha'ul alludes. The identity of this truth, that is, God's plan through the Messiah, has now been revealed much as a Jewish bride is unveiled on her wedding day.

3:4

If you read what I have written –

The Greek participle implies the public reading of the Scriptures that was (and still is) common practice in the synagogue service. Undoubtedly the early messianic congregations continued the practice of public readings of

49

the Torah followed by the reading of the Haftarah (selected readings from the Prophets). Not only were they to be read publicly but also these Scriptures are chanted in the ancient melodies as instructed by Moses (cf. Deuteronomy 31:19). Although there are some musical variations as a result of the various cultures among Jews, the melodies of the *trope* (cantillation) are consistent worldwide.

It is commonly understood that when people sing a passage they actually doubly reinforce its meaning by using both sides of the brain. No wonder God commanded such a practice! The New Covenant reveals that the Messianic believers also followed the synagogue order of service. To these traditional readings they naturally added readings from the New Testament Scriptures as they had developed. Those public readings of the New Covenant are alluded to here as well as in other references such as Colossians 4:16 and Timothy 4:13.

3:6

Gentiles were to be joint heirs, a joint body and joint sharers with the Jews –

The mystery of God is, in the larger sense, the plan of redemption through the work of Messiah. An important sub-set of that plan is that Gentiles will be equally accepted in this plan of messianic blessing. Rabbi Sha'ul again is quite careful to be abundantly clear with his readers. The Gentile believer does not replace the Jewish believers in this plan but shares in their spiritual blessings. He does not say they have become the only heirs but that they are jointly receiving these blessings with the Jewish remnant.

50

The non-Jews are not described as starting a new religion or new exclusive community but they are now jointly part of the eternal plan of one spiritual body with their Jewish brothers. Neither are the Gentiles said to be taking over the promises of God but jointly sharing these blessings with the Messianic Jews. Please note that this does *not* include aspects of the physical covenant (like the Land of Israel as promised to Abraham and his Jewish descendants), but rather the spiritual blessings associated with the other aspects of the covenants.

There is no room to see Sha'ul as an advocate of replacement theology or supersessionism as is common in some religious groups today. Some teaching even appropriates the blessings for Christians while leaving the curses for the Jews! When correctly understood, the teaching of Rabbi Sha'ul reinforces the unity between Jew and Gentile. It also explains that Gentile believers now get to share some Jewish blessings.

As the illustration of the previous chapter shows, the *m'chitzah* (barrier wall) has come down so the Gentiles can come into Jewish space (2:14). Thankfully there are more and more Gentile believers today who understand their connection to the Jewish roots and show their love for the Jewish people. Have you pondered your spiritual blessings lately? What have you done to return the blessing to Israel and the Jewish people?

3:8

To me, the least important –

As the Emissary reflects on the wondrous mystery of Messiah, he cannot help but remember God's gracious call in

51

his own life. It would have been enough for this Jewish man to come to realization of Yeshua as the true Messiah. Yet Sha'ul was not just your average Jew. As one of the zealous rabbinical students of Gamliel, he had risen to lead the "Anti-Yeshua Committee" to snuff out this perceived heretical Jewish sect. But an amazing thing happened on his way to Damascus when he encountered the risen Yeshua! Going from a persecutor to a proclaimer, Sha'ul had a deep appreciation for God's grace. He humbly admits that he clearly did not deserve such an honor of being part of Messiah's Kingdom.

3:9

Letting everyone see…this secret plan –

Rabbi Sha'ul also rejoices in his calling to bring this same Good News to the Gentiles. In an amazing way, God called this traditional Jew to bring the light of salvation and the Scripture to the dark pagan world. It is not so strange, however, when one reflects on the many promises of the Tanakh that the light of the God of Israel would ultimately be shared worldwide through the Jewish people (cf. Genesis 12:3; Isaiah 49:6). This secret plan (mystery) is therefore nothing new but Sha'ul exults in the fact that this plan is now being implemented through the work of Yeshua as Messiah.

3:10

The Messianic Community –

Perhaps most surprising is the visible manifestation of this plan of God; that is, the Congregation in Messiah. The Greek word here (*ekklesia*) is often translated as the word "church", but this can be confusing. For most people (Jews and non-Jews alike), a church is a house of worship for non-Jews while a synagogue is a place for Jews. However as one goes back 2000 years, it is understood that the "ekklesia" in this context was simply a community of Yeshua-followers. Many have forgotten the very point that Sha'ul is trying to make; that the mystery of the *ekklesia* (*kehilah* in Hebrew) is that the Gentiles would be brought in to fully participate in the spiritual blessings of Messiah. This is the revelation of the Messianic Community through Yeshua's work. It is a multi-cultural entity which is inclusive of all tribes and tongues who embrace Yeshua, the promised Redeemer. Consequently, there will be a multitude of cultural expressions in this universal Body and all cultures are to be respected. Yet it is ironic that many people fail to understand that Jewish followers of Yeshua usually desire to maintain our God-given heritage through the expression of a messianic synagogue. The mystery of the *ekklesia* is not that the Jews will convert to a new culture but that the Gentiles will join the Jewish believers in partaking of Messiah's riches. In reflecting over these truths, Sha'ul rejoices in the eternal wisdom of God's plan.

3:12

We have boldness and confidence –

This incredible truth has a practical application in the life of the believer. For the non-Jews, there was a newfound access to the God of Israel, now their Heavenly Father. What was so remote in the pagan religions is now a reality through Israel's Messiah. They have been brought close to God and have a new confidence as they trust in the redemptive work of Yeshua.

Contemporary Bible-believing Christians should also have a heart of gratitude for this truth.

By using the first person plural, the Rabbi also acknowledges that even those who are Jewish enter a new reality through the work of Mashiach. There were always some barriers that kept even the most religious Jews at a distance from our God (cf. Isa. 59:1-2). The early Yeshua movement included tens of thousands of Jews who had experienced a new, closer walk with God and a confidence not previously experienced. In Yeshua's own words: "I have come so that they may have life, life in its fullest measure" (Yochanan/John 10:10).

The Rabbi's Prayer for Love (3:14-21)

3:14

For this reason, I fall on my knees –

At the end of this amazing theological presentation of the early chapters of Ephesians, Rabbi Sha'ul stops for a prayerful reflection. Jews are not commonly known to pray or worship from the knees but it is not unheard of. Daniel was said to pray from his knees as he interceded for Jerusalem (cf. Daniel 6:10). Even in a few modern synagogue services on *Yom Kippur* (the Day of Atonement) there is a dramatic moment during the *Aleinu* prayer when the Cantor lies prostrate on the floor. It is a physical expression of one's need for humility and submission to the plan of God, especially on this High Holy Day. Sha'ul here shows such submission and praise for the unveiling of God's unique plan in sending the Messiah for all mankind.

3:16

The treasures of his glory –

By sending the Messiah, God has opened up the treasure trove of his eternal riches. These are now the inheritance of every Jew and Gentile who calls on the name of Yeshua. The treasures of redemption and abundant life now reside in the inner spirit of each believer. Above all, the Rabbi prays that they will be founded in love, the central message of the Torah. A story in the Talmud illustrates this truth as well.

One day, a non-Jew who wished to know the condensed message of the Torah approached the great Rabbi Hillel. To make it simple he requested that the Rabbi give his answer while standing on one foot. Hillel answered him "What is hateful to yourself, do not do to your fellow man" (Tractate Shabbat 31a). Yeshua gave essentially the same answer but in the positive form, the Golden Rule (cf. Matthew 7:12). Either way, the foundation of all the Scripture and the God of Israel is love and this is the call to all of God's children as well.

3:18

To grasp the breadth, length, height and depth of the Messiah's love –

Even with all the riches that Messianic Jews and Messianic Gentiles have experienced, the Emissary prays that we will continue to grow in our understanding of it all. It is in fact beyond our full knowledge in the *olam hazeh* (this present age), but we are exhorted to strive to be filled with all the fullness of God. Wherever we are in our spiritual journey, we can always grow. Spiritual growth is in fact the sign of one in

55

true relationship with Yeshua. It is at the same time daunting and yet exciting, as our relationship with God should never be stale or static. We should ask ourselves if we're making progress and growing in our personal relationship with God through Yeshua?

3:20

Able to do far beyond anything we ask or imagine –

Sha'ul exults in prayer with the reality that the God we worship is all-powerful and able to accomplish anything that is according to his divine will. Not only that, but our Father is able to do things even beyond what we may ask or even imagine. Messianic believers have a relationship with the Omnipotent Father who loves to work all things for good for his children. Many times these things are even beyond what we may ask him in prayer. This is not to say that we always understand the challenges that come to us in life. Yet he is the One who knows better what is really the best answer for every situation. How much easier it is for us to not push our personal agenda and to trust our loving Father.

3:21

To him be glory…forever –

The Rabbi concludes his prayer of thanksgiving with an acknowledgment that there will be glory given to God for all these gifts. It is not just the reflection of the last few verses that leads him to this but a survey of all the blessings of God reflected in the first three chapters of this letter. God's divine plan of world redemption through the Messiah is beyond reproach. Humanity may have caused much pain and suffering in history, sometimes even in the name of religion. But God cannot be blamed for such actions. The tragedies of human history are actually proof that mankind has not followed the truth of the Scriptures.

No matter about the confusing issues of the world, the Rabbi here reminds us all that God will ultimately work all things for good and certainly for his glory. This glory is experienced by those who diligently seek him *l'dor l'dor* (from generation to generation), a hope expressed in the siddur (the Jewish prayer book). To this important truth, Sha'ul simply closes with the Hebrew exclamation "*amen.*" God is the Faithful One!

CHAPTER 4

"Let your house be a meeting place for the rabbis, and cover yourself in the dust of their feet, and drink in their words thirstily"

(Pirke Avot 1:4)

Using our Gifts for Messiah's Kingdom 4:1-16

4:1

Therefore –

The letter to the Ephesians now reaches a major transition. In the first three chapters Rabbi Sha'ul essentially lays the solid theology for the growing Yeshua movement. He is careful to cover such vital topics as redemption, power and the mystery of the Gentiles now joining the Jewish remnant in this spiritual journey. The word "therefore" ties the upcoming teaching to these earlier concepts. Yet the Rabbi will focus on the practical impact of the Good News of Messiah. How does this message impact our congregations, marriages, families and general relationships in this present age? Chapters 4-6 give the Ephesian believers practical counsel which is still highly relevant today.

I, the prisoner –

We are again reminded that Sha'ul is not giving this teaching from the comfort of his home or rabbinical academy but from the confines of a Roman prison. His practical exhortations therefore are not just religious platitudes but heartfelt lessons honed within the harsh reality of the present world. The recipients of the letter would no doubt pay extra attention to this emissary who did not just talk the walk, but also walked the talk! Ephesians is often joined with other similar letters penned by Sha'ul during his years of confinement and are sometimes called, "The Prison Epistles" (Philippians, Colossians and Philemon).

Lead a life worthy of your calling –

It has been clearly documented how, through the work of Yeshua, all believers have been chosen for a new purpose and perspective (cf. 1:4). We have received an amazing inheritance through the riches of this new life. Yet the Rabbi felt the need to exhort his disciples to live up to these high privileges. If we have truly trusted in the person of Yeshua, then we can be confident that we are in fact the spiritual children of God. But kids do not always act in the best way! Our goal now, as God's own children, is to live up to his Name and to make our Father proud. In Jewish theology, this concept is called "*Kiddush HaShem* (Sanctifying God's Name). We will always be his children through the work of Yeshua, but what kind of children are we? Are we living up to our high calling in Mashiach? Are we making God's Name, his reputation, look good?

4:2

Always be humble, gentle and patient –

The call to humility should be a natural response to the truth of the previous sections. The believer in Yeshua has so many blessings, all gifts from the Father. If all spiritual blessings come through God's grace then one must strive to live with this perspective. The exhortation to be gentle echoes back to the teaching and example of Yeshua himself (cf. Matthew 5:5). The biblical concept of gentleness is often misunderstood to mean meek or even weak. Yet it was Yeshua, the manifestation of YHVH, who was the epitome of gentleness. A correct understanding of the word shows that it means a strong person who is in control of his spirit. The word for patience implies longsuffering and endurance under difficulties. Rabbi Sha'ul was evidently learning many of these lessons during his unjust imprisonment. He appeals to his readers to cultivate this patience in the midst of some of their own difficulties as they lived in the pagan community of Ephesus.

Bearing with one another in love –

If God has shown so much mercy to us, how much more so should we bear with the frailty of others. Once again the Apostle points out the centrality of love as the fulfillment of the Torah and all the Scriptures (cf. Romans 13:10). It is significant that he does not use one of the common words for the love found in Greek, such as *phileo* (brotherly love). But he uses the word for the unique, unselfish love (*agape)* that is now to be central in our lives as Messianic believers.

While the Tanakh often speaks of walking in love (cf. Deuteronomy 6:5), the teaching of Yeshua and the New

Covenant indeed raises the standard to new heights. This kind of idealized, unselfish love can only be attained through the love of God that is now shed abroad in our own spirit. As noted above, not only is the experience of personal salvation a gift from God but also the indwelling of the Ruach, which enables us to have the adequate power beyond our own ability (cf. 2:8-9).

4:3

Preserve the unity –

Sha'ul does not exhort the Ephesian believers to walk in unity. They were already modeling that in their community. What he does feel the need to write is a reminder to protect the unity that already exists. The *Shaliach* had commended them earlier on one of the greatest pictures of unity: the unity between the Jewish and Gentile believers in Yeshua (cf. 2:19-22). Such spiritual unity does not require uniformity. In fact the manifestation of this shalom between diverse groups of believers is a strong testimony to the power of the Good News. Here Sha'ul reminds the Ephesians that such unity must not be taken for granted but must be actively strived for to maintain.

4:4

One body and one Spirit –

If people have a problem walking in unity with fellow believers, they are missing some basic truth of our faith. We are all part of the same body of Messiah. The writer uses an informative analogy to communicate this truth. We are not merely members of a certain congregation. Nor are we merely adherents to the same religious philosophy. No, when a person puts personal trust in Yeshua as Messiah, he is said to become part of a living organism. If the fingers are not in unity with the arm, there will be trouble! Add to this the fact that, when people receive the Messiah, they receive the *Ruach* (Spirit of God). It should be easier to preserve the unity when we realize that we are actually spiritual brothers and sisters, born of the same Spirit (cf. I Corinthians 12:13).

4:5

One Lord, one immersion, One God, the Father of all –

It would be natural in Rabbi Sha'ul's mind to speak of Yeshua as the one Lord. The term is so common that many today simply talk of Yeshua as Lord, that is, the King. While this is true, the term *kurios/Adonai* is so much deeper in Jewish thought.

The personal name of God (*YHVH*) was known and used in the Priestly service of the ancient Temple. The Talmud explains, "In the Sanctuary the Name was pronounced as written; but beyond its confines a substitute Name was employed" (Tractate Sotah VII.6). Even without the vowel points, which were not added until 900 C.E. (A.D.), the correct pronouncement of the name was known because of its daily use. However with the destruction of the *Beit Ha-Mikdash* (Temple) in 70 C.E., the priestly service ceased and, after several hundred years, the exact pronunciation was lost to the Jewish community.

Jewish custom dictates that instead of trying to guess at the correct pronunciation, in deference to the third commandment, we use a substitute term like *HaShem* (The Name) or *Adonai* (Lord). Since Sha'ul here is referring to Yeshua, he attributes to him the divine nature of YHVH. The term Adonai is not just Lord but the substitute term for God Himself. This is just one of the multiple times where the New Testament equates Yeshua with the divine revelation of YHVH (cf. John 1:1, 14; Philippians 2:6-11).

Likewise, the Messianic believers of Ephesus experienced the same immersion. There is only one immersion in water in the name of Yeshua (cf. Matthew 28:19). There is also an immersion of the Spirit, a common experience for all those who trust Messiah (cf. I Corinthians 12:13). Both of these emphasize the reason for the unity among all believers. Believers, irrespective of their different denominations, all have the same Father, the God of Israel. He is the only God, the Creator of heaven and earth, who rules over all. We have every good reason to preserve the wonderful unity purchased by the Messiah!

4:7

Each one of us, however, has been given grace –

God has provided his redemption to us through his grace but that is not where it stops. He has also equipped us with a gift drawn from the bounty of Messiah. The Greek word for grace, *charis*, is the same word used to describe our experience of Yeshua's salvation (cf. 2:8). As our redemption is a free gift of God, so too is this grace gift a free present from the Father. In recent decades there has been a focus on the "charismatic" gifts of the Spirit. This is an important aspect of our faith but it should be noted that here it is emphasized that every believer in Messiah has a certain *charisma* (grace gift) for service in his Kingdom. The verse here implies that we are given differing abilities based on the various levels of Messiah's equipping. Although the gifts vary, Rabbi Sha'ul is quick to point out that each believer without exception is the recipient of at least one grace gift.

4:8

This is why it says...he gave gifts –

The Emissary highlights a parallel passage from the *Tanakh* that predicts the bestowing of the *charis* (grace) gifts. The original context of Psalm 68:18 speaks of King David, after a victorious military campaign, giving gifts or spoils to his troops. Some literalists might object to the apostle's use of this passage in the context of spiritual gifts. However, as a trained Pharisaic rabbi of his day, Sha'ul is making use of some common interpretive methods used within first century Judaism.

It was summarized by the acronym "PARDES" which means garden or paradise. The four Hebrew letters however stand for the following: Pey/P for *peshat* (literal interpretation), Resh/R for *remez* (allusion), Dalet/D for *darash* (illustrations) and Samech/S for *sod* (hidden). In this verse, Sha'ul is making a nice rabbinic point by the use of *remez*, an allusion to Messiah through the experience of King David.

4:9

Now this phrase, "he went up" –

Sha'ul now explains his application of Psalm 68 to the work of Messiah. If Yeshua "went up," the clear implication is that he must have descended before that. In a midrashic understanding, Yeshua descended to the earth in his incarnation as he took on human form (John 1:1, 14). The Gospel writer implies that this event fulfilled the symbolism of the holiday of *Sukkot* (Feast of Tabernacles) as "the Word lived (tabernacled) with us." The Messiah subsequently "went up" to the Father at his resurrection from the dead on the third day of Passover as is pictured in another

Jewish holy day called *Bikkurim* (First Fruits). See Lev. 23:15; I Cor. 15:20. This is a good reminder why Messianic Judaism continues to observe the Torah calendar and holy days. They contain spiritual lessons that all believers should appreciate. The Rabbi continues his illustration by teaching that at this point, after his ascension to the Father, Yeshua gave gifts to his people for the equipping for service in his Kingdom.

4:11

Some as emissaries, some as prophets, some as proclaimers –

Sha'ul now enumerates the specific spiritual gifts that are given to Yeshua's followers. The gift of being an **emissary** is for those sent out to represent Yeshua. In Judaism it has a much stronger meaning than merely one sent out. It also means a direct spokesman. The Talmud says, "a *shaliach* is the same as the one who sends him" (Tractate Berachot 34). As was noted previously, this would obviously include the original twelve emissaries chosen by Yeshua but also other sh'lichim who were sent out on various tasks (cf. 1:1).

The gift of serving as **prophet** is seen in two different but related ways in the Scripture. First, the gift describes one who can foretell future events, which was a unique element of the prophets of Israel. The Hebrew Prophets made many astounding predictions that came to pass. This is actually the required test of a true prophet of God: 100% accuracy. Anything less led to serious consequences in ancient Israel (cf. Deuteronomy 18:20-22). However, a *navi* is not just a futuristic predictor, but also one who can declare God's truth in general. The Jewish prophets, even with their unique predictions, had a lot more to say by way of exhortation, rebuke and encouragement. All this is implied with the spiritual gift of prophet.

There may be predictive elements (which should be carefully tested by the Scriptures) but at times God equipped some believers with a gift to proclaim the truth of God in a clearer manner. Most Messianic Jews believe in the existence of the spiritual gifts as listed here and elsewhere in the New Covenant. Even if there are differences of interpretation, it is clear from the Scriptures that great care must be taken to use the gifts as God intended. In I Corinthians 12 and 14 there are many details. It is not coincidental that chapter 13 on "love" is in the middle!

Proclaimers of the Good News is listed as another essential gift for the body of Yeshua. Every believer is called to share the Good News of Yeshua with all those around him (cf. Matthew 28:18); yet, God has equipped some individuals with an unusual ability to effectively proclaim this Good News. What a blessing to see this gift at work even today through the Messianic movement!

Some as shepherds and teachers –

The Hebrew word for **shepherd** (*roeh*) evokes a most beautiful picture. From ancient times, the duties of a *roeh* would include feeding, protecting and guiding. Of course some sheep go astray on their own perilous path and need rescue (cf. Psalm 23). Sha'ul notes that God has equipped some within the body of Yeshua to fulfill the job of a spiritual shepherd, a vital calling since the sheep of Messiah need to be watched over. The Greek syntax here makes a direct connection between the shepherds and teachers. It could even be considered one gift of teaching-shepherds. Either way, the importance of good teaching cannot be over-estimated in the spiritual life. Sha'ul lists the gift of teacher as a vital ingredient to our spiritual well being. In the Jewish community we call our clergy, "rabbi," which reflects the great emphasis on teaching. We are thankful for the many Messianic Rabbis in our modern movement who are using this spiritual gift to teach the flock of Yeshua, both Jews and Gentiles, in the ways of God.

4:12

Their task is to equip God's people –

So important is this gift of teacher/*rabbi* that Sha'ul gives more details of their job description. Most rabbis do a large part of the work of ministry but that actually is not to be their top priority. How much more effective it is when the rabbi equips the local community who in turn performs the details of the ministry! This profound statement, when acted upon, will save the local rabbi and staff from burn out. It will also naturally open the door to other members of the local congregation to be blessed as they do the work of the ministry for Yeshua! The results of this balanced philosophy of ministry will be that all the members of the body of Yeshua will grow in faith and become mature participants in his holy work.

4:14

No longer infants –

In contrast to the previous description of maturity, the believers are urged to grow up beyond their spiritual infancy. The analogy is an apt one as the spiritual life is often described in parallel terms of physical development. As with one's physical birth, there is also the need for a spiritual birth. This was the point that Yeshua discussed with another famous rabbi of the first century (cf. John 3:3). After one's birth there is the time of growth. An infant moves from the crib, to crawling, then to toddling, as he begins walking. It is this analogy that Rabbi Sha'ul brings in his word of exhortation. The Ephesian believers, both Jewish and Gentile, had been born of the Spirit but time had come for them to move beyond spiritual infancy. It is understandable for a baby to throw some of his food off his plate but it is totally shocking to see a grown adult do the same thing! Yet, there are Yeshua believers who never grow beyond their baby stage. The Rabbi wants his people to know that they can all grow up.

Blown along by every wind of teaching –

There is a note of irony in the Rabbi's exhortation. He had just highlighted the importance of good teaching and good shepherds for the believers in Yeshua. But evidently some of them were all too willing to accept some teaching that was not correct. They are said to have opened themselves up to "clever people" who were skilled at deceiving the ignorant. As a result of not listening to good teaching, they found themselves blown along like a ship in a storm. The waves were causing them to be tossed around as they lacked the sure foundation of good teaching from the Scriptures.

4:15

Instead, speaking the truth in love –

In contrast to the deceptive message of the false teacher, the Ephesians are exhorted to abide in the truth of Yeshua and the purity of the Good News. This truth is not only good for their own spiritual life but it is to have a positive impact on those around them. What is the basis of this "truth?" A rabbinic midrash illustrates it well where it is pointed out that the word "truth" (Heb. *emet*) comes from the letters that are first, middle and last in the Hebrew alphabet (*alef, mem,* and *tav*). This is said to be a reminder that all truth comes from God, the first, middle and last in all things (Genesis *Rabba* 81.2).

Yes, we must communicate the truth of God, but in a loving manner. It does no good to berate people with the truth. We might drive them further away. But our calling is to not compromise the truth of God as we let it shine through our loving spirit. We need both elements in balance: truth and love. By so doing, the Apostle says that we will grow up in the Messiah.

4:16

Under his control, the whole body –

The spiritual body of Messiah is fitted together in such a way as to be beneficial to us and to bring glory to God. He is the one who gives the required gifts and holds us all together. He even provides the nutrients for the healthy movement of his body, down to the very joints of the skeleton. When we do things God's way, Sha'ul says that each part will fulfill its intended function and result in a strong spiritual body.

As if to emphasize the point, the Rabbi asserts that love is the main building block for the body of Yeshua. This is an important word for the first century Messianic believers of Ephesus, as vital in our own day!

Are we growing in our faith with Yeshua? Have we moved beyond the baby stages of our spiritual life? Have we discovered our spiritual gifts and are we using them within a local messianic synagogue or congregation? May we, like the Ephesians, receive the teaching of Rabbi Sha'ul and apply it in a dynamic way as we press on with Messiah!

The Pagan Lifestyle or Messianic Renewal 4:17-32

4:17

Therefore...do not live any longer as the pagans live –

Although Jewish believers from the local synagogue had birthed the Messianic community of Ephesus, many new believers from the Gentile community soon joined them. In the first century, Gentiles were involved with rampant paganism. The only way to break free of that lifestyle was to affiliate with the Jewish people and the God of Israel. Consequently, a number of former pagans became either God-fearers or full converts to Judaism. With the arrival of Yeshua and the messianic fulfillment, there was now another viable option.

Gentiles were now invited to equally participate in this New Covenant faith and thus be directly connected to the God of Israel (2:11-16). Rabbi Sha'ul exhorts these non-Jewish followers of Yeshua to not revert back to their former lives. They now have a higher calling and purpose as a result of their redemption and placement in the community of faith. Of course it is a reminder to the Messianic Jews of Ephesus as they too could succumb to the temptations of the pagan world. All believers in Messiah must stay vigilant in their focus on maintaining a godly walk.

Their sterile ways of thinking –

71

The word "sterile" means empty or aimless and is an appropriate description of the pagan lifestyle. If a person has no relationship with the living God, then what is his purpose? Ultimately, there is no point to all the effort, time and resources put into seeking the meaning of our lives without being connected to our Creator. Many are aimless and empty today and thus try to fill the void with all sorts of worldly substitutes. Some things are obviously destructive like bad relationships and addictions. Others may even be good things like commitment to career or putting our faith in good relationships. Ironically, some people even use religious observances in their quest to find true meaning. They are all inadequate substitutes for a real relationship with God. Messiah has come to connect us to the source of all blessing and peace. Our lives are restless until we make that connection with God.

4:18

Their intelligence has been shrouded in darkness –

The world places great value on academics and information. It all sounds good and convincing to the multitudes, but once again it is a deception. As *Shlomo* (Solomon) reflected on this, he concluded that "the fear of Adonai is the beginning of knowledge"—*Mishlei* (Proverbs 1:7). The wisdom and knowledge of the world is no doubt impressive, but it pales compared to knowing God. There is spiritual deception that can take place when we seek intelligence without the knowledge of our Father in Heaven. Ironically, Sha'ul even calls such intelligence "ignorance," as the pagan values of the world actually resist God's will.

4:19

Practicing any kind of impurity –

This is a natural result of a mind and heart far from God. Once again the context of this letter to Ephesus is informative. The city was the headquarters for the Roman Temple of Diana, one of the seven wonders of antiquity (1:1). The Romans had embraced the Greek goddess of fertility (Artemis) and rebranded her for their purposes, which included sexual immorality. The sentence implies that there is a progressive inability of the conscience to do its work as a person keeps resisting the truth of God. There is a danger in such a case that one's heart and moral values will become calloused, much like Pharaoh's did in ancient Egypt. It is even more difficult at that point to understand and discern the will of God.

As the mind and heart turn away from the values of God, the bad fruit in the person's life becomes obvious. The Rabbi notes a short list of examples including sexual immorality and greed. As a traditional Jew, Sha'ul had a high view of the Torah, the instruction of God. There are many aspects to the Torah/Law but part of it was to keep Israel on the right track.

Rabbinic tradition notes that there are two main sections of the Torah: 248 positive commandments and 365 negative commandments, which together comprise the 613 total *mitzvot* (laws) in the Torah. 248 is said to be the number of bones in the human body and 365 represents every day of the solar year. Hence, we are called to perform the commandments every day with all our being (Tractate Makkot 23b). In contrast, the pagans walk in such a way that breaking the

Torah commandments is a habit. They would by definition be considered "impure" in a ritualistic sense and forbidden to come close to the things of God.

4:20

Not the lesson you learned –

Rabbi Sha'ul gives them the short but powerful reminder that this is not the walk of redemption learned from the Messiah. He emphasizes that this new life must be learned. It does not come naturally or without concerted effort. We must be students of the Torah and all the Scriptures. Most importantly, we must consistently apply the truth of the Word in our daily lives. The pressure of the pagan world will invariably press hard on all believers but we will stand strong as we actively grow in our spiritual lives. The Talmud gives a beautiful illustration of the relationship between rabbi and disciple when it says, "Let your house be a meeting place for the rabbis, and cover yourself in the dust of their feet, and drink in their words thirstily" (Pirke Avot 1:4). We are to stay so close to our rabbi that his dust covers us. That means not getting too far behind Yeshua or too far ahead of him! Sha'ul reminds his readers, including us, that we must continue to learn and apply our Rabbi's words to guarantee our spiritual victory in this world.

4:22

Strip off your old nature –

The analogy here is that of changing clothes. The old way of life is compared to some old clothes that do not suit us anymore. In fact they are called thoroughly rotted! It is also analogous to the *yetzer ha-ra* (evil inclination), which unfortunately has too much control over us. Once again the Rabbi reminds the Messianic believers of Ephesus that there is great deception when we yield to the evil inclination. So many people are blissfully walking on the wide path to destruction! This is the way of the pagans and it used to be the way of many of the Ephesian believers in their pasts. But they now have a new calling and purpose in Yeshua, which necessitates new spiritual attire.

4:24

Clothe yourselves with the new nature –

The new clothing includes a renewed mind and spirit. It is not merely washing the old clothes, as it were. The Messianic faith is not just a self-help or self-improvement program. It, in fact, is just the opposite. Yeshua did not call his disciples to merely improve the self but to die to self (cf. Matthew 10:38-39). The new clothes referred to actually represent an entirely new nature. This new spirit and new heart are predicted in the *Tanakh* as a benefit that God will provide in the days of Messiah (cf. Ezekiel 36:24-28; Jeremiah 31:31-34). The believers of Ephesus had experienced this renewal when they trusted in Yeshua as their Messiah which, in turn, produced fruit that is opposite of the pagan world. In contrast to the *yetzer ha-ra* they are now producing fruit consistent with the *yetzer ha-tov*/the good inclination. Sha'ul notes that it is righteousness and holiness that flow from the truth of Yeshua.

4:25

Therefore, speak truth –

Paul continues to enumerate the various fruits of a truly renewed life. In previous situations they were tempted to lie and misrepresent the truth. But that is now unacceptable in the Messianic walk. They must speak the truth with each other, especially since they are intimately related as spiritual brothers and sisters. All behavior should now be a *Kiddush Ha-Shem* (a sanctification of God's Name).

4:26

Be angry, but don't sin –

It is commendable to be angry in the right situation. Anger itself is not always a sin. The quote is actually from the words of King David as he speaks of righteous indignation (cf. Psalm 4:5). Yeshua himself expressed anger but never sinned. He manifested a righteous anger over the injustice in the Temple Courts (cf. *Yochanan*/ John 2:13-17). Some people object to his action, but even the Talmud confirms that the Jewish public considered many of the priests of the first century ungodly.

Of special note is a reference to "the bazaars of the sons of Annas" which corrupted the sanctity of the Temple compound and how they "beat the people with staves" (Tractate Pesachim 57a). It is indeed right to oppose all forms of injustice. The problem is that we mortals often confuse righteous indignation for the unrighteous anger of our fallen spirit. Hence, here is the exhortation to refrain from sin despite an expression of anger.

Moreover, the Rabbi counsels believers to not let the sun go down before the cause of the anger is dealt with. This is sage advice. Unforgiveness has a terribly destructive effect on one's soul. It has been said that holding a grudge is similar to taking a poison pill and waiting for the other person to die!

Unforgiveness can be devastating to the spiritual life, and that is not the worst of it. Such sin opens the door for the Adversary to maximize the damage. Such a situation should motivate believers to deal with any ungodly anger that may enter their spirit.

4:28

The thief must stop stealing –

The grammar of the verse suggests that some of the Ephesians struggled with this past sin. Believers in Yeshua are to turn from any such behavior and make an honest living by their own efforts. There are to be no *shnorers* (moochers) in the community of Messiah. Each individual is to perform an honest job to provide for themselves and their family. Instead of the previous life of thievery and taking advantage of people, the newer believers are told to even share with those in need. It is reminiscent of the Torah injunction to leave the corners of your field in order to share your blessings with the less fortunate (cf. Leviticus 19:9-10). Not surprisingly, the body of Messiah is to conduct itself with many of the same principles already given to Israel in the Torah of Moses.

4:29

Let no harmful language come from your mouth –

Sha'ul concentrates a special focus on a problem area for many people; that is, our words. Since most of the Ephesian

77

believers originally came from the pagan world of the Roman Empire, this would be a timely reminder. Fallen society usually does not think twice about the use of inappropriate or hurtful words. In many places it is actually part of the accepted culture or even considered a sign of strength. In Judaism, and now in the messianic community, it is to be otherwise. Our words reflect the real condition of our spirit and we are to use them wisely. For example, what is considered one of the worse sins is *lashon ha-ra* (speaking evil of others). A graphic reminder in the Tanakh is the account of Miriam and Aaron speaking against Moses along with the resulting judgment (cf. Numbers 12).

Even if there is some truth to a statement, one is encouraged to hold back his or her words if they are not edifying. The Talmud even takes it further in an interesting discussion of this topic. It is said that we should even be wary of negative, non-verbal communication. It is called *avak lashon ha-ra* (the dust of evil speaking) and includes such actions as rolling the eyes, nodding in approval or spreading innuendos. How interesting that we can be influenced by the negative dust of evil speaking or by the positive dust of our rabbi (4:21)!

The principle of avoiding *lashon ha-ra* (evil speech) obviously carries over to the listener as well. The Talmud sums up its perspective in the following: "Why do human fingers resemble pegs? So that if one hears something unseemly, one can plug one's fingers in one's ears" (Tractate Ketuvot 5b). Rabbi Sha'ul's exhortation is not only to avoid that which is hurtful but also to speak words that will be a benefit to others. Such language will not be destructive or even neutral, but will build up those who hear. In short, we have enough negativity in the pagan world. We certainly don't need it in the community of Messiah! Is our language uplifting or negative? Are people encouraged or discouraged when they are around us?

4:30

Don't cause grief to God's Ruach HaKodesh –

It is bad enough that hurtful language has a negative impact on others. But such behavior also hurts the Ruach who lives within the believer. If we aren't motivated to better speech on account of those around us, then we should give thought to the fact that God himself might be hurt in the process.

4:31

Get rid of all bitterness, anger, and slander –

The *Shaliach* ties this exhortation to the fact of the Ruach's presence in our lives. The renewed life includes all facets: words, thoughts and actions. Whatever is ungodly and produces negative fruit, we are told to dispose of. These things not only hurt others but they greatly hinder our own spiritual journey. Don't we have enough challenges without dragging an extra backpack filled with cement? We are admonished to get rid of the extra weight so we may more fully enjoy God's blessing in our life.

4:32

Instead, be kind, forgive each other, just as in the Messiah –

In contrast to the problematic attitudes of the old nature, the Messianic believers are encouraged to put on that which makes for edification. Instead of tearing down, we are to build up. Despite the temptation to hang onto negative attitudes, we are to let them go in the spirit of forgiveness. Some may object to this high standard, as it seems virtually impossible within our own strength. That is why the Rabbi immediately ties these positive attitudes to the work of Yeshua on our behalf. If God has shown great kindness to us, how can we not treat others the same way? If the Father through Yeshua has forgiven us of our own transgressions, do we have any legitimate basis not to show sincere forgiveness to those around us? Those who understand the grace of Messiah are the ones who find it easy to extend that same kind of grace to others. We should ask, How is our own spiritual journey progressing? Are we having more and more victory over the *yetzer ha-ra* (evil inclination)? Do people see in us the good fruit of a life submitted to the Ruach? May we continue to walk in the abundant life provided through Yeshua our Messiah!

CHAPTER 5

"Did you transact your business honestly? Did you fix times for the study of Torah? Did you fulfill your duty with respect to establishing a family? Did you hope for the salvation of the Messiah? Did you try to deduce one thing from another in study? Even should all these questions be answered affirmatively, only if "the fear of the Lord is his treasure" (Isaiah 33:6) will it avail, otherwise, it will not."

(Tractate Sanhedrin 31a)

Filled With the Ruach 5:1-20

5:1

So imitate God, as his dear children –

Rabbi Sha'ul presses on with some important counsel for his disciples in Ephesus. In the previous verses he has given many detailed instructions on how to walk in the new life with Yeshua. He now gives a summary illustration of the motivation for following these religious commandments.

Since the Ephesians were now God's children, they should imitate the actions of the Father in Heaven. One of the first instincts of children is to naturally follow the example of their parents. A child may not always know the reason for a certain

81

behavior but it will seem logical to follow the parent who is doing the training. So, too, in our own spiritual lives. We may not know all the 613 *mitzvot* (commandments) or other important details, but if we try to imitate our Father we will not be far off the path.

5:2

Walk in love -

Once again the Rabbi points out that love (Gr. *agape*; Heb. *ahavah*) fulfills all the demands of the Torah. Love does no wrong to others and thus is the central requirement of any commandment. By using the Greek word *agape* the readers are reminded that this is the kind of unselfish love exemplified in the life of Yeshua. He gave himself as an offering through his death thus fulfilling the typology of the *korbanot* (sacrifices) of the Temple. Like the *korbanot*, this sacrifice produced a pleasant fragrance to the Father who was pleased to receive this act (cf. Leviticus 1:9). Since Messiah has shown so much unselfish love, the least we can do now is imitate God's love to those around us. In this case, the saying "like father, like son" is a worthwhile goal.

5:3

Among you there should not even be mentioned –

If we are now walking in the love of Messiah, many things will by definition be excluded from our lives. It is inconsistent for the children of God to be caught up in sexual immorality. The Greek word *pornea* used here, includes any sexual relations outside the holy covenant of biblical marriage (pre-marital sex, adultery, homosexual lifestyle, even pornography). What was often acceptable in the pagan Roman Empire has no place in the life of the Messianic believer. It should be noted that the

Torah and New Covenant never condemn the person himself but it is the breaking of Torah that is to be avoided.

Sha'ul reminds his disciples elsewhere that many of them even came out of some of these lifestyles, being transformed by the power of the Ruach (I Corinthians 6:9-11). Just to show that he is not merely focused on sexual sins, Sha'ul also lists here any kind of impurity or greed that was also easily observable in the city of Ephesus. The followers of Yeshua have a new calling and purpose. It won't be easy but they are exhorted to let the *yetzer ha-tov* (good inclination) have victory over the desires of the *yetzer ha-ra* (evil inclination).

5:4

Also out of place are obscenity and stupid talk –

Our words are a reflection of the thoughts of our heart. Vulgar words and coarse language do not reflect the light of God. As Messianic Jews and Gentiles, the Ephesians were called to use edifying speech and to give thanks. A note to help explain the intention of the verse is to realize that all the forbidden actions are stated in the present tense of the verb. These are not just people who slip into a foolish action or word once in a while. These actions are said to be ongoing and a habitual lifestyle. Such people live this way as a way of normative life, unlike the follower of Yeshua who at least battles to stay on the narrow path.

5:5

Has no share in the Kingdom of God –

This is a sobering statement that needs serious reflection. Torah and the entire Scriptures not only impact this life but also the world to come. While Judaism has placed great value on the concept of *Tikkun Olam* (Repairing the World), we dare not neglect the world to come in the process. Rabbinic teaching stresses the great importance of walking in God's ways as a prerequisite of entering the future Paradise. This is such an integral part of our relationship with God that the Apostle warns not to let anyone deceive us into thinking it's not. Especially in pagan society, many would seek to assure us that all is fine even if we live a lifestyle that is displeasing to God.

This passage reflects the reality of the balance needed between the actions of this life and the world to come. Yeshua reminded his disciples of the foolishness *of gaining the whole world and yet losing your own soul* (cf. Matthew 16:26). It is a valid concern: have we placed our hope only in the salvation of the Messiah, or do we realize that our lives still need to be a pleasing aroma to God to be assured of our blessing in the World to Come.

5:8

You are light –

The Rabbi now switches to a common analogy of the first century Jewish community. The contrast between light and darkness was established early in the creation account of the Torah. The order of creation takes an unusual turn as it states, "So there was evening and there was morning, one day" (cf. Genesis 1:5; also 1:8, 1:13, etc.). The pagan orientation started with the light of day and proceeded into the darkness of night. So, the sun itself became a focus of the pagan religions.

In contrast, the Jewish people were told that the day starts in darkness but moves to the light. The tradition is that it begins when three stars are observed in the sky. This is an apt spiritual analogy as God is moving the dark world to the light of his Kingdom.

In first century sectarian Judaism, the Qumran Community perceived itself as "sons of light" in the midst of spiritual battle with the "sons of darkness" (cf. War Scroll 1QM). It would be natural for Sha'ul to refer to the messianic believers of Ephesus in a similar fashion. Although they were formerly associated with darkness, they now were filled with light as they connected to the Messiah. Their walk should therefore reflect the light of God.

5:10

What will please the Lord –

In keeping with the overall theme of this chapter, Sha'ul admonishes the believers to imitate their Father (5:1). Here the Ephesians are challenged to live like children of light. It is important to point out that they already are children of light through their relationship with Yeshua. But now they are told to live up to that high calling. The fruit of the light includes goodness, rightness and truth. They are called not just to take a minimalist view of their faith but they are to maximize it by seeking to please their Father in Heaven. Too many believers today seek the minimal requirements of their faith. Yet God is looking for those who go the extra mile to do things that are well-pleasing to him.

5:11

But expose them –

Instead of walking in the darkness of the world or being apathetic to it, Yeshua's disciples are called to actively shine the light. Darkness is an appropriate image as many of those deeds are even too shameful to discuss. They are done in secret for a reason. But light reveals the true nature of all these things.

The darkness of society can be discouraging and many times even overwhelming. But as the old saying goes, "We can either curse the darkness or light a candle!" The Rabbi quotes this principle from a compilation of verses in the Tanakh to prove his point. In *Yesha'yahu* (Isaiah) 52:1 the prophet calls on Zion to awaken and put on holy garments. Likewise, in *Yesha'yahu* (Isaiah) 60:1 he calls on Jerusalem to arise, "For her light has come." Some interpreters may question Sha'ul's inclusion of "the Messiah" as the source of the light but he is making use of the classic midrashic method commonly found in rabbinic interpretation (4:8). It is clear that Yeshua is the Light in every Messianic believer's heart. This interpretation by the Apostle confirms the Jewish background and education of the writer.

5:15

Therefore, pay careful attention –

The *Shaliach* calls on the believers of Ephesus to live wisely. Too many people are walking aimlessly and hurting their own lives with foolish choices. We must use wisdom as we walk with God in this confusing world. Since the fear of Adonai is the beginning of knowledge, believers are directed to seek the ways of God found in Mishlei (cf. Proverbs 1:7). This wisdom will not come naturally or without effort. The best way for believers to have the wisdom of God is to saturate ourselves in his Word. Instead of letting the world mold us, we will then be able to let the Ruach and the Word renew our minds for walking in the blessings of Yeshua (cf. Romans 12:1-2). Even our time on earth is to be used wisely as it is an important stewardship given to each of us by our Father in Heaven.

5:17

What the will of the Lord is –

The Father has certain hopes and aspirations for his children, most notably that we would all walk in his good plan for our lives. The will of God would include all the areas discussed by Sha'ul, such as our speech, our thoughts and our actions. We have a basic choice every day: will it be the values of the world or the will of the Lord we follow? The Rabbi has already discussed many important details in regards to our personal walk with God. He will now address the implications of the messianic life in such areas as marriage, family and our work.

Biblical faith is not just meant to be a religion expressed only in a house of worship. It is also eminently practical as we apply the wisdom of God to every aspect of our existence. The New Testament, not surprisingly, follows the Jewish approach. It takes a holistic perspective of life and faith. The first century Greek philosophies compartmentalized aspects of life into separate categories, for example, religion was distinct from work. The Gnostics even drew the division so strongly as to say that the soul is good but anything material is innately evil.

Unfortunately, many "religious" people today have the same Greek attitude of not mixing their spiritual faith with their everyday life. The biblical view is that all comes from God and we are stewards of his gifts. It is summarized in the

Shema prayed three times daily by observant Jews: "You shall love the Lord your God with all your heart, all your being and all your resources" (cf. Deuteronomy 6:4-9).

5:18

Don't get drunk with wine –

Rabbi Sha'ul addresses the topic of God's will by first looking to the source of one's power. Many in the Ephesian congregation, being largely from a pagan background, had experienced the power of alcohol. While not condemning the use of alcohol per se, the Scriptures are clear in condemning the abuse of alcohol or other addictive elements (cf. Proverbs 20:1). Drunkenness is an awful thing in itself but it also represents a larger picture of being controlled by something beyond oneself and God's Spirit.

5:19

Instead, keep on being filled with the Spirit –

The Rabbi makes both a comparison and a contrast in the same verse. In contrast to being drunk, messianic believers should seek to be filled with the Ruach of God. Why turn to artificial stimulants like alcohol or drugs when we can tap into the very power of God? There is also a comparison to the Ruach and drunkenness in that both speak of something controlling a person. The word "filled" speaks of the wind as it fills a sail. It is a perfect picture, as the word for wind and spirit is the same Hebrew word, "ruach." It is also an apt description, as a boat must go where its sail captures the wind. Instead of a one-time action, the filling of the Ruach must be a continuous, daily event. Those of us who trust Yeshua must continuously seek to walk in the power that already resides in us. As has been said, we don't need more of the Spirit but the Spirit needs more of us!

Psalms, hymns and spiritual songs –

The believer who allows the Ruach to take control of his or her life will manifest several other phenomena. Most notably the person will have a new love and appreciation for worship. Rabbi Sha'ul underscores this fact as he connects the filling of the Spirit with one who loves the various forms of worship. The Psalms are in essence the first Jewish prayer book. Many were joyfully expressed through instrumental music and even folkdance (cf. Psalm 150). The Greek translation even means "striking fingers on a string." The term "hymns" means a song of praise about God's character. The term "spiritual songs" has a slightly different emphasis as it focuses on the believers experience and personal testimony. Since the Apostle is writing before the destruction of the Temple in 70 C.E., he knew firsthand the beauty of the Jewish worship service. It wasn't until post-70 C.E. that music and dance ceased, as a sign of mourning the Temple's destruction. Many modern Jewish synagogue services are slowly reinstating some of these ancient forms. How appropriate that the Messianic Jewish synagogue movement should be leading the way in joyous music and folkdance. Since the Messiah has come, we cannot help but be joyful in our worship services! This is truly the fruit of the Ruach in our heart.

To each other…to the Lord…in your heart –

This new appreciation of worship starts in the heart of the Spirit-filled believer but must overflow beyond that.

From earliest times, the Jewish expression of faith has taken place within the larger community. It is that larger group that makes it possible for us to fulfill many of the mitzvot of the Torah. It is very difficult, if not impossible, to live Jewish biblical faith in isolation. Sha'ul alludes to this here as he exhorts the messianic believers to express their worship "to each other." It is true of course that God is always with his children, even in isolation. But it is the same God who says it greatly pleases him to see his children come together for this holy purpose.

5:20

Always give thanks for everything –

Another natural fruit of the Ruach is thankfulness. As the Ruach reveals more and more of what God has done, we are filled with thanks. The Talmudic rabbis encouraged every person to say a minimum of 100 *berachot* (blessings) each day (Tractate *Menachot* 43b; see 1:3). This would have a positive impact on our thinking and perspective. Rabbi Sha'ul takes it to an even higher level, as we are to give thanks for everything. By keeping our eyes on Yeshua, the Ephesians and us today should be the most positive people on God's earth!

To God the Father in the name of our Lord Yeshua the Messiah –

Rabbi Sha'ul once again states his theology in a very Jewish way. God is addressed as our Father in Heaven innumerable times within Jewish liturgy (*Avinu Malkeynu, Av HaRachamim*, etc.). Rabbi Shaul does not change this format but adds a vital element, in the name of Yeshua, the divine Mediator (2:18). In the Semitic world, a name was more than a mere ID tag. It is often descriptive and even prophetic of a person. Hence, to pray in the name of Yeshua is to call on the Father through the work of his Son. The Messiah can be the source of our prayers at times but he himself emphasized that he came to be the bridge between us and our Father in Heaven (cf. Yochanan/John 14:6). Yeshua is of course the expression and divine essence of YHVH but his role is primarily to mediate the gap that normally divides us from God.

Messianic Marriage 5:21-33

5:21

Submit to one another –

Rabbi Sha'ul now turns his attention to a most practical application of his teaching about the Spirit-filled believer—the covenant of marriage. Unlike the ancient pagan societies the Ephesians were part of, Judaism and the Bible have always held the highest regard for this relationship. It is said in the earliest verses of the Torah that it is not good for man to be alone. This is magnified in importance when one remembers that Adam was in a perfect paradise created by God. Yet something essential was missing, so God says, "I will make for him a companion suitable for helping him" (cf. Genesis 2:18). *Ezer kenegdo* is the Hebrew phrase that literally means "a helper that is against him." Certainly it is not desirable for the wife to be in total opposition to her husband, but it seems true that God's companion for man will be one very different from himself. It is often true that opposites attract. We don't need a spouse who is exactly like us but one who fills in our weak spots. Ultimately, the religious definition of marriage is

91

spelled out as the following: "A man is to leave his father and mother and stick with his wife, and they are to be *basar echad*, "one flesh" (cf. Genesis 2:24).

It must be noted that the biblical marriage relationship is more than a mere convenience of secular society but it is actually a binding spiritual agreement with stipulations. It was in the dark days of the Prophets that many of Israel's sins were listed. Among them is this: "Adonai is witness between you and the wife of your youth that you have broken faith with her, though she is your companion, your wife by covenant" (cf. Malachi 2:14). In Talmudic Judaism, the covenant of marriage is considered so holy that it is actually called by the name *Kiddushin* (Sanctified Marriage). An entire tractate of Talmud, *Kiddushin* deals with the important laws pertaining to marriage and the responsibilities of the husband and wife.

All this is background for the exhortation of the present verse in Ephesians 5:21 where the *Shaliach* calls all believers to submit to one another. The word "submit" (*hupotasso*) has often been misunderstood to mean to allow oneself to be oppressed without complaining, even in the midst of a true injustice. But the term literally means "to arrange under" or "to fit in order." Submission in the Bible is not to suppress but actually results in just the opposite where the person finds God's perfect order for them! Sha'ul uses this concept to begin an extended section on interpersonal relations in the messianic community.

5:22

Wives should submit to their husbands –

With an understanding of *hupotasso* (submission) in mind, it must be noted that this command does not place the wife in an inferior role. All people, regardless of their positions in life, are equal in standing before God through Messiah (cf. Galatians 3:28). The world may place a greater or lesser value on persons as was true in the first century Roman Empire. In that world (and still in some places today), wives were considered as property and also greatly inferior to their husbands. The Rabbi encourages the wives to be in correct biblical submission—not subservient but a complement, equal to her husband.

Wives were always given great social status in Judaism as illustrated in the following rabbinic quote: "Honor your wife, for thereby you enrich yourself. A man should be ever careful about the honor due to his wife, because no blessing is experienced in his house except on her account" (Tractate *Bava Metzia* 59a). It is therefore logical that the New Testament affirms their distinctive role in marriage. Women have many gifts. The mothering instinct not seen in most men is something unique to women. In a connected theme, Sha'ul also exhorts the Messianic wives to respect their husbands. Men often look for this in the marriage relationship and women should be motivated as they realize they are actually showing respect to Messiah in the process (5:33).

5:23

Husband is head of the wife just as Messiah, as head of the messianic community –

Sha'ul will have more to say in regards to the role of the husband but the overriding principle is stated here. The husband is called to be a leader in his marriage and family, but this is not to be understood in normative terms. Headship means dictatorship in some marriages, but Scripture explains

93

that the husband is to be the head of the family as a servant leader. This is emphasized as the writer shows that the husband is to exemplify Yeshua himself. He came as a leader by serving others, even to the point of his self-sacrificing death on the Roman cross. This is clearly the greatest example husbands have and clearly defines the biblical idea of headship in marriage. Hence, the Rabbi encourages the wives to submit to their husbands even as they submit to Yeshua.

5:25

As for husbands, love your wives, just as the Messiah loved the Messianic Community –

While the wives are called to fit into God's plan for them, the husbands receive a stronger exhortation. This letter puts a great deal more responsibility on the husband's role (nine verses for the husband compared to three for the wife). The overriding teaching for the husband is to "love your wife." Rabbi Sha'ul uses one of his favorite words, "love," the same type of love illustrated through Messiah and shown by his concern for his people. Just in case the husband needs some extra motivation, Paul points out that since the husband and wife are one, he is actually doing something good for himself, also. It is as if the husband is blessing himself when he blesses his wife.

In Jewish tradition, there is a very practical way for a husband to show appreciation for his wife. At every Shabbat dinner, after the blessing of the candles and on the bread and wine, there is a special blessing for the wife. The husband reads or sings the well-known verses in Proverbs 31:10-31, called, *eshet chayil*, a "capable, virtuous wife." Even if the week was hyper-busy, it is a beautiful moment where the husband acknowledges the special gift of his wife. Not only are husbands called to be servant/leaders; they are also called to bless their wives in a priestly way.

5:26

Set it apart for God –

The Rabbi is no doubt alluding to the Jewish name for the marriage covenant—*kiddushin* (sanctified marriage). It is an illustration that every Jew would understand. As biblical marriage is a consecration of a woman to a man, so, too, it reminds us of our being set apart as a people for God. In fact, the phrasing of 5:26-27 (and the broader context of Ephesians) is reminiscent of the entire Jewish wedding ceremony. (See *God's Appointed Customs* for more on the Jewish/biblical wedding).

Making it clean through immersion in the mikveh –

Here the Rabbi makes another reference to the *mikveh* (immersion pool) as he discusses family purity laws, specifically in the Jewish wedding traditions. It was and still is a common practice for a Jewish groom and bride to take a ritual immersion in water at a mikveh just before the final step of their wedding. Rabbinic law dictates that a kosher (acceptable) mikveh must have at least 200 gallons of rainwater funneled into the pool. Each natural body of water (oceans, rivers, lakes, etc.) is already considered an acceptable mikveh. We find immersions in Scripture (cf. II Kings 5; Matthew 3).

It should be noted that a person must be thoroughly clean before being totally immersed, thereby showing that the waters of the mikveh are not for physical cleansing, but for a spiritual purpose. In Jewish sources the act of *tevilah* (immersion or baptism) is akin to "being born anew."

One interpretation of the mikveh relates it to an experience of death and resurrection, and also to the reentry into the womb and reemergence. Immersing fully, you are like the fetus in the womb, and when you come up out of the mikveh you are as reborn. The individual who has sinned and become impure is transformed; he dies and is resurrected and becomes a new creation, like a newborn child (Buxbaum, *Jewish Spiritual Practices*, p. 569; also the words of Yeshua in Yochanan/John 3:3).

Rabbi Sha'ul makes an important point here by alluding to the custom of mikveh on one's wedding day. It is the responsibility of the new husband to make sure both he and his bride take this symbolic immersion as they start their lives together. This beautifully parallels the immersion of the Ruach that makes all believers ceremonially clean as we open our hearts to the Messiah.

Sha'ul emphasizes both aspects within the Jewish wedding customs. In a literal sense, Messianic husbands are to mentor their wives in the spiritual life so they are clean and without defect. Similarly, we believers are called to live as faithful brides and to partake of this mikveh in anticipation of our wedding day with Messiah. In so doing we will be a spiritual bride that is holy and cleansed, waiting for him.

5:31

Therefore a man will leave his father and mother and remain with his wife –

Rabbi Sha'ul again refers back to the early verses of the Torah and God's design for marriage. Yet he takes it a step further in reminding husbands to be godly leaders in their marriages. It is all illustrated in the Jewish understanding of marriage and the final step of the Jewish wedding ceremony called *Nisuin* (Full marriage).

As the one-year engagement time draws to a close, the Father of the groom initiates the last part of the ceremony with the sounding of the *shofar* (ram's horn). The general community (and even the bridal party) never was sure of the exact time, so they needed to always be ready (cf. I Thessalonians 4:13-18; Matthew 25:1-13). At the sound of this shofar, the wedding procession would begin from the groom's home to pick up the bride to bring her to the *huppah* (wedding canopy). There, the *Ketubah* (written contract) would be signed and vows exchanged. The second cup of wine would be shared along with the seven blessings over the couple. At the completion of the ceremony, the couple would now be fully married and could live together with full conjugal rights.

Today, almost all the above elements are included in one ceremony in the modern Jewish wedding. They still speak volumes about our relationship with God and his plan for the future. Messianic Jews and non-Jews have become "engaged to Yeshua." We currently await the sound of the shofar announcing the return of the groom, King Messiah, and to start the final wedding processional.

5:32

There is profound truth hidden here –

The final step of the Nisuin also contains symbolism about our personal relationship with God. A good Messianic marriage shows mutual love and respect; so does our relationship with God. At some point the Father will have the *shofar* (ram's horn) sounded to call all believers to the final step of our wedding ceremony. The marriage of the Lamb, as it is also known, will include another cup and many blessings to represent this final stage of our marriage to the Messiah.

At Yeshua's Last Seder, he declared that he would not partake of the fourth cup until he sees his people again in the Kingdom (cf. Matthew 26:30). This will also be followed by the greatest Jewish wedding reception ever (and that is saying something)! True followers of Yeshua will then be reunited with him to live together in the 1,000 year Messianic Kingdom centered in Jerusalem. What a time of rejoicing that will be!

Husbands, are we fulfilling our roles as servant leaders to our wives and family? Wives, are you living up to your high calling of being a suitable complement for your husband? The Jewish wedding teaches us today. We have all received the invitation to this joyous event. Have we sent in our RSVPs by receiving Yeshua as our redeemer? He desires for all people to attend this great Jewish wedding.

CHAPTER 6

"The world only exists through the breath of schoolchildren. We may not suspend the instruction of children even for the rebuilding of the Temple."

(Tractate Shabbat 119b)

Messianic Children and Parents 6:1-4

6:1

Children, obey your parents –

The Rabbi continues with his theme of submission. He now turns his attention to the obvious connection between children and parents.

Some child rearing takes a hard line. The parent is the authoritarian "boss" and there is no room for dialogue with a child. However, such views minimize or totally misunderstand the biblical view of submission. As was taught above, the word translated, "submission," is *hupotasso*. It does not imply either inferiority or superiority, but literally means, "to arrange in order." Everyone has a role and position to serve in God's order of things. Husbands and wives are co-equal partners yet with distinctive roles to play in the marriage. So, too, children are taught that they have a particular place in God's order.

As with all people, children are to be respected as those created in the image of God. But there is an authority structure that, when followed, is a blessing for both children and parents. In this case it is the children who are to obey their parents; if the order is reversed it leads to chaos.

Although all kids may challenge this arrangement from time to time, the fact remains that most of them greatly appreciate the stability that comes from it. Too many kids in modern society are acting out in damaging ways because they lack the example of two godly parents. Children will find it easier to obey the family boundaries when they sense the love of God through the love of their parents.

Some adults err by over-indulging the wants and desires of the children, whereas some don't show much grace at all. It is not easy for parents to strike a balance between appropriate authority and flexible grace, but the Rabbi challenges his readers to try.

In union with the Lord –

This phrase can be understood in a number of ways. Some may think this is an exemption clause. While this interpretation may apply, the grammar allows for another understanding.

The phrase "in union with the Lord" may apply not only to believing parents, but also to the child. In other words, it is the child's own Yeshua-faith that should lead him to follow God's design, irrespective of the status of the parents.

Either way, this verse is not implying that children must obey their parents at all times. The exception to this "rule," is if the guidance is sinful or ungodly. Ultimately, children are called to obey God even above parents if necessary. Of course it is God himself who calls on kids to show obedience to their parents. The Rabbi does not give a lot of justification for this command but merely says, "This is right." It sounds odd to our relativistic society but the Torah is still a tree of life to those who embrace it (cf. Mishlei/Proverbs 3:18). Children will be blessed, as they understand the wisdom behind this structure of the family.

6:2

Honor your father and mother –

Sha'ul offers another reason for kids to follow this exhortation. It goes all the way back to one of the Ten Commandments. *Kibud av va-eym* (Honor your father and mother). It is in fact the first commandment with a promise attached to it. The Torah says that things will go well for those who follow it and that they will live long in the Land (cf. Exodus 20:12). God gives a blessing to those who apply his Word. A happy family life is worth pursuing!

6:4

Fathers, don't irritate your children –

After the exhortation to the Ephesian children, the Rabbi addresses the responsibilities facing fathers. First is the prohibition against irritating or provoking their children. Kids may not perfectly live up to God's standards, but it is also a sobering reminder that dads can stumble as well. Children might become angry or internalize the anger with depression. They may act out or be inappropriate. But a deeper analysis looks at the environment of the home as well and dads play a crucial role.

We can even be the source of the provocation of our son or daughter and for that, God holds us accountable. Instead of irritating our kids, the Messianic dad is admonished to raise them up in the Lord's environment. Sha'ul says that this includes discipline which will include boundaries for acceptable behavior. It is related to the term "disciple" and a father's first disciples must be in his own home.

We would like to believe that our kids will naturally behave, but world history proves otherwise! Children, when left to their own devices, often make the wrong choices. It is hard to blame them too much since they lack life experience. That is why Shlomo (Solomon) exhorts the parents of his day to "train up a child in the way he should go" (cf. Mishlei/ Proverbs 22:6). Messianic dads must be concerned enough about their kids to correct their bad behavior and give them proper boundaries for a successful life.

Therefore, the father should be the servant/leader of his family, especially in regards to teaching and reading the Word. The *Shema* reminds dads that they are to talk of godly values when they are traveling down the road or sitting at home (cf. Deuteronomy 6:4-6). The implication is that Messianic dads are not just to speak the Torah but, more importantly, to model the Torah. In fact, a great deal of spiritual damage can be done if dads speak the Torah without walking the Torah.

There is another way in Jewish tradition for fathers to bless their children...literally! At every Shabbat dinner, after the blessings over the candles and challah, there is a blessing over the kids. For the boys it is the biblical blessing found in Genesis 48:20: *Yesimcha Elohim k'Ephraim u-Manasheh* (May God make you like Efrayim and M'nasheh). Over the daughters we say: *Yismeych Elohim ke-Sarah, Rivkah, Rachel va-Leah* (May God make you like Sarah, Rebekah, Rachel and Leah). Not only do our kids receive the benefits of these powerful words but every Shabbat we fathers get to show our appreciation for them. Instead of irritating our children, fathers can encourage them in the ways of Messiah. Dads, are we living up to our sacred duties?

Bosses and Employees 6:5-9

6:5

Slaves, obey your human masters –

Sha'ul's use of the word "slave" should not be confused with the oppressive version of slavery that plagued some societies (like the U.S.). In Judaism, slavery was an acceptable form of servitude, used by a person to voluntarily pay off some debt. Instead of modern bankruptcy laws, a Jewish slave could choose a master that suited him as he sought to improve his life situation. Jewish slaves were even guaranteed many rights from their Jewish master. Among these rights would be just treatment and even a limited time of servitude (seven years) until one is set free at the *Shmita* (Sabbatical) year.

To illustrate the positive nature of slaves within Israel, the Torah even states that sometimes a slave would not want to leave his benevolent master! To prove his allegiance, the slave in such cases was commanded to have his ear pierced on the door of the house (cf. Exodus 21:1-6). Roman slavery of the first century was significantly different but also included some protective rights. A modern reader of Ephesians would better understand this passage, if the terms "slaves and masters" were replaced by "employees and bosses."

With this context in mind, the *Shaliach* gives the following recommendations. Slaves/employees are to obey their masters/

bosses. Such obedience does not imply inferiority but is in keeping with the idea of biblical submission, that is, fitting into God's order (5:21). Bosses and workers may stand as equals before God but it would wreak havoc in the workplace if there were no order. In fact, the writer points out that the workers are to obey with the same kind of respect they have toward the Messiah. Messianic believers should be known as some of the best employees, which in turn may open up some good discussions about perspectives on life.

6:6

Don't obey just to win their favor –

Rabbi Sha'ul reminds the Ephesian believers that their work attitude has a direct impact on their future blessing in the Kingdom of God. Slaves had an obligation to work hard, their responsibility. And the "free man" should also be an excellent employee even though he could opt out of his current job. The Rabbi concludes saying that whoever does good work will be similarly rewarded by the Lord.

Like the Ephesians, we are to work diligently with no ulterior motive. We should be excellent employees because it is the right thing to do in the sight of our true "Boss." Consequently, our good behavior is not just on display when people are watching us. The mature believer understands that he or she is serving Yeshua. Thus, the labor is sincerely from the heart. One definition of integrity is "being righteous when no one is watching." But the reality is that our King Messiah is always watching so we should have the highest motivation for the best work ethic.

Do our co-workers appreciate our labor on the job? Can our boss see our sincere effort to be a blessing to others? Most

104

importantly, is our true Boss, Yeshua, happy with the work that we accomplish in his Name?

6:9

Masters, treat your slaves the same way –

The overall context of the entire passage applies here as well. Masters or bosses might be tempted to ride roughshod over the rights of their employees, as was often the case in the Roman society. But such is not the case in the community of Messiah. Even bosses are to walk in the attitude of submission to Yeshua. Bosses are warned not to threaten their employees as is so common in the world. Masters should keep a balanced approach as they remember that they actually work for the same boss as their slave. Such a work environment will actually decrease stress and help build a positive atmosphere that will often help the business prosper, especially under God's blessing.

The Spiritual Battle 6:10-18

6:10

Grow powerful in union with the Lord –

As Rabbi Sha'ul begins ending his letter, he feels compelled to address an essential topic for the messianic believer—the spiritual battle. He has already firmly established the point that this current world is often a hostile place for those who seek to walk with God (2:1-3). The environment of this age is often chaotic and destructive since its principle ruler is Satan. There are so many things that transpire in day-to-day life that are not the perfect will of God. It was a dangerous thing for God to give mankind freewill and the tragic fruit is seen in the daily news. It is within this hostile environment that the follower of Yeshua finds himself.

The result is an ongoing spiritual battle between the forces of evil and the power of God. It may seem overwhelming, but Sha'ul is not totally pessimistic about the battle. We are already more than conquerors through the work of Yeshua and the ultimate victory is guaranteed! Yet the battle rages for those who seek to walk in the light of God's ways. For this reason the Apostle reminds his readers to grow strong in their faith-walk. He has already commended the Ephesians on their remarkable spiritual growth and success as followers of Yeshua (1:13-16). But as is often the case, he also exhorts them to grow even stronger in the Lord. The snares of the fallen world are way beyond their own strength to overcome, but with God's help, they will find their way to final victory in Messiah. The strength of God is offered to every believer in the midst of worldly challenges.

6:11

Use all the armor...that God provides –

Since this battle is in the spiritual realm, by necessity it requires special weapons. While Rabbi Sha'ul will use the analogy of a soldier, he clearly is referring to the spiritual armor of God. The following details can fit the description of a Roman soldier of the first century, but there are some intriguing variances from spiritual armor. It is more likely that, as a Rabbi, he is referring to spiritual weapons that would be understood in the context of Judaism. God has provided these weapons, not the Israeli army. In fact it is essential that we use these spiritual weapons to stand against the spiritual forces that oppose God.

106

Against the deceptive tactics of the Adversary –

The Adversary is Satan. This phrase is even a play on words, as the Hebrew word Satan means opposition or adversary. Although he was originally one of the angels close to the throne of God, he chose to oppose his Creator and even led a rebellion of other angelic beings. Most commentators agree that the descriptions of a fallen pagan king can only be attributed to a greater spiritual power, Satan (cf. Isaiah 14:12-17; Ezekiel 28:11-19; Revelation 12:1-11). Consequently, it is not an earthly king, but Lucifer (a later Latin translation) and his demons that were cast out of heaven to the earth where they continue to cause spiritual havoc (2:2). This is not just a Christian teaching but it is also well documented in rabbinic theology as well.

It is said that the work of Satan falls into three broad categories: he seduces mankind, he accuses them before God, and he inflicts the punishment of death (Tractate *Bava Batra* 16a). It was Satan who was responsible for encouraging Israel to make the Golden Calf in the wilderness (Tractate *Shabbat* 89a). As his name implies, Satan is constantly opposing all that God seeks to establish. What makes this spiritual war especially tricky are the deceptive tactics that are employed by the Adversary. Satan knows that most people would recognize his destructive ways if he made a direct attack. He is much too deceitful to appear in the obvious red leotards with the pitchfork of legend! He is more likely to cause his confusion through guerilla warfare or surprise attacks.

Rabbi Sha'ul warns elsewhere that Satan will even disguise himself as an angel of light (cf. II Corinthians 11:14). No doubt the Adversary will seek to attack humanity in its areas of greatest weakness, whether it is greed, illicit sex, addictions, or even religion! Tragically, he does a pretty good job of keeping unbelievers distracted and away from the Kingdom of God. However, here the Rabbi is addressing the believers in Messiah and warning them to be on the alert. Satan knows he cannot recapture the true believers in Yeshua (cf. John 10:28-29). But the Adversary can certainly get believers off the good path of walking with Messiah. It is not a question of losing one's salvation but losing many of God's intended blessings. For this reason, the Apostle warns the believers to stay alert and to keep armed with spiritual weapons.

6:12

Not struggling against human beings...but against spiritual forces of evil –

With all the craziness of the world, it is tempting to blame external sources. Yet, while all people are accountable to God for their attitudes and actions, those who have some spiritual discernment understand that it is not just an outward battle being fought. All these evils are merely manifestations of the greater spiritual battle that is taking place.

Most of the world scoffs at the idea of the existence of Satan but the fact remains that someone is doing a very good imitation of him! In fact it is evil spiritual rulers, authorities and cosmic powers that are stirring up so much trouble.

Even if most of the world is in denial, the Scriptures, as well as the ancient rabbis, confirm that there are spiritual forces that are manipulating the events of world history. As the *Shaliach* says, it is a spiritual struggle of epic proportions.

6:13

So take up every piece of war equipment God provides –

The Rabbi has informed the believers to use the right spiritual equipment for this battle. Here is a more specific exhortation for them to take up every piece of battle gear. God has already provided what is needed but what good does it do if it stays in the storage locker? This is precisely the point where too many Messianic believers of today fail. Many feel defeated and beat up by the Adversary because they have not taken up their battle gear. It must be an active choice combined with exerted effort on our part. We are called to resist and to stand firm. This is the difference between a defeated, confused Messianic believer and a believer who is walking in strength and victory! No soldier would think of going into battle without his armor. As with the Ephesian believers, we too must make use of every piece of equipment that God has provided if we are to be victorious in our spiritual lives.

As noted earlier, it would seem reasonable that Sha'ul is referring to the equipment used by the ubiquitous Roman soldiers in the city of Ephesus, an apt analogy as one considers a military battle and the needed equipment. However, there is another good analogy. Sha'ul will now quote a number of references in the Tanakh to back up his teaching, the bulk of which deal with the garments of the High Priest of Israel. These garments, spoken of in the Torah, have a great application to the battle in the spiritual world (cf. Exodus 28:1-4).

6:14

Have the belt of truth buckled around your waist –

Some of the following biblical quotes not only apply to the *cohanim* (priests of Israel) but to the ministry of the Messiah himself, the Great High Priest! For example, the first piece of equipment is said to be "the belt of truth." Such a belt or sash would be essential equipment for both a soldier, as well as a Jewish priest. A soldier would need a belt to make sure his garments would not be a hindrance in battle. On the biblical side, this fact is found in the common expression "to gird your loins" which meant to tie up the loose clothing so you have unhindered work. Such a belt would be required for the intense work of the priest as well. The Torah speaks of a sash, made of fine, blue linen (cf. Exodus 28:39-43). The sash was practical, and also symbolized the spiritual calling of the Levite—to work for the heavenly kingdom. As his proof text, Rabbi Sha'ul quotes a passage about the belt of truth worn by the Messiah, when he comes to rule Israel (cf. Isaiah 11:5). We, as his followers must have truth as our belt if our warfare is to be unhindered.

Righteousness for a breastplate –

The next piece of equipment could also relate to both a Roman soldier and a Jewish priest. For a soldier, the breastplate was most essential to protect the vital organs while in battle. If the heart or lungs are injured it would most likely mean a fatal end. In a different way, the breastplate of the priest was essential for protection as well. In his case it was not so much the physical organs of the body but the spiritual essence of the soul. In Judaism, the heart is symbolic of the inner being of every person and it needs protection.

Not surprisingly, the Torah requires the High Priest to wear a *choshen* (special breastplate) to symbolically protect his heart as he ministers. The breastplate was an important reminder of a critical ministry of the *Cohen Ha-Gadol* (the High Priest). It contained twelve different stones representing the twelve tribes of Israel (cf. Exodus 28:15-21). The Cohen was to always be a mediator between God and his people, a perfect picture of the priestly ministry of the coming Messiah. The Rabbi quotes a verse from the Tanakh that alludes to this breastplate and the fact that it represents the righteous character of God himself (cf. Isaiah 59:17). The battle of the Spirit cannot be fought with a Roman breastplate, but requires the spiritual breastplate represented in the Cohen Ha-Gadol. As we believers enter spiritual battle, we need to protect our souls with the righteous breastplate of God.

6:15

Wear on your feet the Good News of shalom –

Roman soldiers were well known for wearing their tough, cleated sandals as they went to battle, essential for good footing while in combat. But here Sha'ul says that the Ephesian's feet should be shod with shalom. In contrast to a Roman soldier, the High Priest did not wear any shoes during his ministry. The original language of this verse reveals that the word "shoes" is not even in the text. But, this is another clue that Sha'ul is primarily thinking of the spiritual weapons given to Israel as opposed to the physical equipment of the Roman army.

Again the Rabbi shows his affinity for the scroll of *Yesha'yahu* (Isaiah) as he quotes the passage speaking of "Good News" being our footwear, instead of shoes (cf. Isaiah 52:7). No wonder the entire message of the *B'rit Hadashah* (New Testament) is called Good News for all people. Yeshua paid the price to bring shalom between all of humanity and his Father in

Heaven. In turn, we are told to go into spiritual battle, not with spiked sandals, but walking in the *shalom* of God.

6:16

Always carry the shield of trust –

A military shield was an important part of a soldier's weaponry. It was a great defense against incoming arrows. The Roman army was known to carry a shield covered in leather, dampened with water. Not only would the arrows be blocked, but also the flames would be extinguished in the process. The High Priest did not have any such shield. However, it was known that God is the shield of defense for all who walk with him (cf. *Tehillim*/Psalm 3:3).

The six-pointed star was used in the Jewish community as early as the first century C.E., but it was not a universal symbol until much later. What is commonly referred to as the "star of David" is in Hebrew called *magen David* (shield of David). This was an appropriate choice for the flag of the modern State of Israel. King David treasured the fact that God himself was his shield.

Rabbi Sha'ul reminds the Ephesians that they need to carry the shield of God in their spiritual battles. Likewise, our trust in Yeshua guarantees our protection from the flaming arrows of the Evil One.

6:17

Take the helmet of deliverance –

A first-century soldier would have a helmet as part of his arsenal. It was essential for protection of the head, the command center for the entire body. On the spiritual front,

God's children need to protect their minds. The *Cohen Ha-Gadol* was instructed to have a special head covering that would symbolize his submission to God and the sanctification of his mind. The word for this means "a protection around the head" which for a soldier would be a helmet. Similarly, the Hebrew word used in Exodus 28 (*mitznefet*) means "to wrap," a requisite element for the priests.

It was probably like a turban or a modern *kefiyah* worn in the Middle East. Most branches of modern Judaism (including Messianic Judaism) encourage men and boys to wear *yarmulke*s or *kippah*s at religious services as a reminder of our priestly calling.

In the spiritual battle, this head covering reminds us to stay submitted to the Father and to let the Messiah renew our minds (cf. Romans 12:1-2). Again the Rabbi references the Prophet Isaiah (59:17) who specifically calls the head covering, "the helmet of *yeshuah* (salvation). God's promise is complete victory for the one who has his mind set on Yeshua!

Along with the sword given by the Spirit –

Of all the weapons given to a soldier, the sword is the only offensive tool. Every other element is for protection against the onslaughts of the enemy. The Roman sword was a feared weapon. How much more so the sword of the Lord!

In the spiritual battle, a military sword was useless. But the Scriptures are called "a double-edged sword (that) cuts right through to where soul meets spirit" (cf. Hebrews 4:12). According to the rabbis, the Torah was said to be the only true antidote to the attacks of Satan (Leviticus *Rabba* 28.3). We cannot bind him up as much as we would like to. In fact, the

Scriptures never exhort us to tie him up but instead, to resist him through the power of the Word of God. Of course our Messiah modeled this for us in his own encounter with Satan. Even Yeshua did not waste his time on curses or magical formulas but quoted the Torah as he drove off the Adversary (cf. Matthew 4).

If Yeshua stood his ground by quoting the Word of God, how much more should we! But how can we use the sword if we are unfamiliar with it? No wonder that study of the Scriptures is one of the highest priorities for the believer. It is a tree of life to those who apply it (cf. Proverbs 3:18)!

6:18

As you pray at all times –

The final weapon of our spiritual armor is prayer. The *Shaliach* points out that it is all kinds of prayer that is essential for our victory. This includes intercession for others as well as praises. Jewish prayer is largely for blessing God (1:15). No doubt prayer, our personal lifeline to God, is a necessary tool in our spiritual battle.

The Ephesians were exhorted to pray at all times. The synagogue or church service is a great time for corporate prayer, but the spiritual battle rages mostly outside of religious services! Believers are encouraged to develop a habit of *tefillah* (prayer) during all our waking hours. In the Jewish world, some have compared the wearing of the *tefillin* (phylacteries used during prayer) to a soldier's uniform in the army of God (Donin, p. 151). It is not unlike the analogy of this passage written by Rabbi Sha'ul. It is a challenge and takes vigilance, but we will be much more likely to succeed in the spiritual life as we stay closely connected to our Father in Heaven.

We are in a spiritual battle, beyond the physical world. If we are to be blessed and fulfilled in our spiritual journey, as with the Ephesians, we must use the resources God has provided. Do we have the belt of truth making our work easier? Are we protecting our heart with the breastplate of righteousness? Are we walking in the *shalom* of the Good News? Do we have our heads covered with the kippah of salvation? Do we pray at all times? This fallen world is a battleground but God has provided the tools for victory and blessings, as we stay connected to Messiah!

Personal Notes From The Rabbi 6:19-24

6:19

And pray for me –

The conjunction, "and," connects what follows to the previous comments. All believers encounter spiritual battles in this fallen world; even the leading Rabbi is not exempt. In fact, Sha'ul probably realized that he even experienced more of that battle because of his important ministry. Sha'ul was a man of prayer and humbly requests prayer on his behalf. It is a beautiful gesture illustrating the close connection between this Rabbi and his readers.

Prayer in itself is a gesture of humility as we call out to God for assistance in things that are beyond our control. The specific prayer of the *Shaliach* is for boldness in making known the secret of the Good News. It was still a secret in most of the Roman Empire, which had little knowledge of the Jewish promises. Likewise, it was still a secret in most of the Jewish community. It would take a special boldness for this Jewish apostle to speak up in the diverse communities where he was being sent. Rejection and physical danger were a distinct possibility. He asked for prayer, as should we.

6:20

Ambassador in chains –

Before Sha'ul could fulfill his calling in Yeshua, he would first need to be released from the Roman prison! The description of his current situation reminds us of the great paradox facing this representative of Messiah.

He is an ambassador, a person with authority to serve in another country. Normally such an ambassador would receive honor, respect and even protection from his host nation. Not so with Sha'ul. Even though he is an ambassador for the Kingdom of Yeshua, he has not been received with open arms in most places. It is ironic: an ambassador sitting in a prison cell! Yet the Rabbi exudes confidence that God still wants to use him despite (or maybe because of) his terrible situation.

We know from other letters that Sha'ul was often chained directly to some of his Roman prison guards. This could have been depressing for him but God reached his "captive audience" through this unusual situation. Evidently, many became followers of the Messiah while watching the renegade rabbi (cf. Philippians 1:12-13; 4:22). The prayers of the Ephesians were efficacious in strengthening Sha'ul for his work as an Ambassador for Messiah.

6:21

Tychicus...will tell you everything –

The Rabbi mentions his personal assistant in his ministry. Since Sha'ul was sitting in prison, it was this believer, Tychicus, who was sent by the Rabbi to deliver and read this letter to the Ephesians. He also was later sent for the same task to the city of Colossae (cf. Colossians 4:7). Sha'ul shows his high regard for this "dear brother and faithful worker for the Lord." Ephesians includes the truth that all believers (not just rabbis, ministers, evangelists, etc.) have a vital function in the body of Yeshua (4:11-13). Tychicus is a great example of one who faithfully used his personal gifts for the benefit of Messiah's Kingdom. He may not be a teacher or a letter writer but he was a faithful assistant to Sha'ul and thus advanced the Kingdom of God.

6:22

He may comfort and encourage you –

Just as Sha'ul was a *shaliach* sent by Yeshua, Tychicus was a *shaliach* sent by Sha'ul. Not only did he faithfully perform his mission of carrying this letter to the Messianic communities of Asia Minor, he also carried personal news as well. It lifted the spirits of the believers to hear that, although their Rabbi was in prison, he was doing well. Perhaps this verse is an indication of the spiritual gifts of Tychicus as he is said to be an encourager. The Greek word, *parakaleo*, literally means, "to be called alongside." Such a person not only feels for others but walks next to them in their time of need. What most people today need is some comfort and encouragement, much like that brought by this Messianic brother Tychicus. We could ask ourselves: Do those around us feel encouraged and built up as we come into contact with them?

6:23

Shalom…love…grace be to you all –

In typical rabbinic fashion, Sha'ul closes his letter with a blessing containing similar themes with which he started (1:1-3).

Shalom is peace but much more. In Greek philosophy, peace is the absence of conflict. In Judaism, shalom also implies health, blessing and true happiness. Certainly the believers of Ephesus would gladly receive this benediction from their Rabbi.

The Apostle also prays that God would give them love and trust. Sha'ul already described the love of God and how it ultimately fulfills all the Torah (4:1-2). Once again the writer uses the unique Greek word *agape* to describe the unselfish love of God. This is why he notes that these qualities can only be given as a gift from God through faith in Yeshua. Grace is also referenced in the closing blessing. The Rabbi's final word to them is that they would never forget the free gift of God and his undying love for his children. Reading this blessing given to the Ephesians, we cannot help but be greatly encouraged in our walk with Messiah!

CONCLUSION

So ends the letter of Rabbi Sha'ul to his friends in the city of Ephesus. It is a great overview of the many spiritual blessings found in the Messiah. The letter is also filled with practical and challenging exhortations on how to apply these truths to everyday lives.

The Ephesian congregation was a diverse group of Jews and Gentiles, united together in Messiah. They experienced many blessings in their own lives and definitely had an impact on the first century world in which they lived. But the Rabbi was not just writing to that local group. What is Paul saying to us?

Through our studies of this letter, may we have a fresh appreciation for all that the God of Israel has done for all people: Jews, Christians, believers, seekers or skeptics. May there be a renewed blessing on our families, our congregations and our communities. May we also have a dramatic impact on the world in which we live through Yeshua, our Redeemer and King!

BIBLIOGRAPHY

Abbott-Smith, G. *A Manual Greek Lexicon of the New Testament.* Edinburgh: T & T Clark, 1973.

Birnbaum, Philip. *A Book of Jewish Concepts.* New York: Hebrew Publishing Company, 1975.

—— ed. *Maimonides Code of Law and Ethics: Mishneh Torah.* New York: Hebrew Publishing Company, 1974.

Boteach, Shmuley. *Kosher Jesus.* Springfield, NJ: Gefen Books, 2012.

Boyarin, Daniel. *Border Lines—The Partition of Judaeo-Christianity.* Philadelphia: University of Pennsylvania Press, 2004.

_____. *The Jewish Gospels.* New York: The New Press, 2012.

Brown, Michael. *Answering Jewish Objections to Jesus (5 Volumes).* Grand Rapids: Baker Books, 2003.

Buxbaum, Yitzhak. *Jewish Spiritual Practices.* Northvale: New Jersey: Jason Aronson Inc., 1994.

Cohen, Abraham. Everyman's Talmud. New York: Schocken Books, 1975.

—— *The Twelve Prophets.* New York: Soncino Press, 1985.

Cohen, Shaye. The Beginnings of Jewishness. Berkeley: University of California Press, 2000.

Cohn-Sherbok, Dan, ed. *Voices of Messianic Judaism.* Baltimore: Messianic Jewish Publications, 2001.

Danby, Herbert. *The Mishna.* New York: Oxford University Press, 1991.

Daube, David. *The New Testament and Rabbinic Judaism.* Peabody, Massachusetts: Hendrickson Publishers, 1956.

Davies, W.D. *Paul and Rabbinic Judaism.* Philadelphia: Fortress Press, 1980.

Encyclopedia Judaica. Jerusalem: Keter Publishing House, 1972.

Epstein, I. (editor). *The Soncino Talmud (CD software).* Brooklyn: Soncino Press, 1995.

Eisenbaum, Pamela. *Paul Was Not A Christian.* New York: HarperCollins Publishers, 2009.

Eisenman, Robert and Wise, Michael. *The Dead Sea Scrolls Uncovered.* New York: Barnes & Noble, 1992.

Fischer, John. *Siddur For Messianic Jews.* Palm Harbor, Florida: Menorah Ministries, 1988.

_____ *The Epistles from a Jewish Perspective* (MP3/DVD series). Clarksville: Messianic Jewish Publishers, 2011.

Flusser, David. *The Sage from Galilee.* Grand Rapids: Eerdmans Publishing, 2007.

Friedman, David. *At The Feet of Rabbi Gamaliel.* Clarksville: Messianic Jewish Publishers, 2013.

Glaser, Mitch. *Isaiah 53 Explained.* New York: Chosen People Productions, 2010.

Harink, Douglas. *Paul Among The Postliberals.* Grand Rapids: Brazos Press, 2003.

Heschel, Abraham Joshua. *God in Search of Man: A Philosophy of Judaism.* New York: Noonday Press, 1993.

Jeremias, Joachim. *Jerusalem in the Time of Jesus.* Philadelphia: Fortress Press, 1988.

Juster, Daniel. *Jewish Roots.* Pacific Palisades: Davar, 1986.

Kasdan, Barney. *God's Appointed Times*. Baltimore: Messianic Jewish Publishers, 1993.

——— *God's Appointed Customs*. Baltimore: Messianic Jewish Publishers, 1996.

____ *Matthew Presents Yeshua King Messiah*. Baltimore: Messianic Jewish Publishers, 2011.

Kinzer, Mark. *Post-Missionary Messianic Judaism*. Grand Rapids: Brazos Press, 2005.

Klausner, Joseph. *From Jesus to Paul*. New York: Menorah Publishing Company, 1979.

Klein, Isaac. *A Guide To Jewish Religious Practice*. New York: The Jewish Theological Seminary of America, 1979.

Lachs, Samuel Tobias. *A Rabbinic Commentary On The New Testament*. Hoboken: Ktav Publishing House, 1987.

Levine, Amy-Jill and Marc Zvi Brettler. *The Jewish Annotated New Testament*. New York: Oxford University Press, 2011.

Neusner, Jacob. *A Rabbi Talks with Jesus*. New York: Doubleday, 1994.

Patai, Raphael. *The Messiah Texts*. New York: Avon Books, 1979.

Prager, Dennis and Telushkin, Joseph. Why The Jews? New York: Simon & Schuster, 2003.

Resnik, Russell. *Creation to Completion: A Guide To Life's Journey From The Five Books of Moses*. Clarksville: Messianic Jewish Publishers, 2006.

Rienecker, Fritz and Rogers, Cleon. *Linguistic Key to the Greek New Testament*. Grand Rapids: Zondervan, 1982.

Rudolph, David and Willetts, Joel (Editors). *Introduction to Messianic Judaism*. Grand Rapids: Zondervan, 2013.

Safrai, Shmuel. *The Value of Rabbinical Literature as an Historical Source (article)*. Jerusalem: JerusalemPerspective.com, 2009.

Sanders, E.P. *Judaism--Practice and Belief 63 BCE-66 CE*. London: SCM Press, 1992.

—— *Paul, the Law, and the Jewish People*. Philadelphia: Fortress Press, 1983.

Scherman, Nosson. *The Rabbinical Council of America Edition of The Artscroll Siddur*. Brooklyn: Mesorah Publications, 1990.

Sigel, Phillip. *The Halakhah of Jesus of Nazareth According to the Gospel of Matthew*. Atlanta: Society of Biblical Literature, 2007.

Soulen, R. Kendall. *The God of Israel and Christian Theology*. Minneapolis: Fortress Press, 1996.

Spitz, Elie Kaplan. *Does The Soul Survive?* Woodstock, VT: Jewish Lights Publishing, 2001.

Stendahl, Krister. *Paul Among Jews and Gentiles*. Philadelphia: Fortress Press, 1976.

Stern, David. *Complete Jewish Bible*. Clarksville: Jewish New Testament Publications,

—— *Jewish New Testament Commentary*. Clarksville, Maryland: Jewish New Testament Publications, 1992.

—— *Messianic Judaism—A Modern Movement with an Ancient Past*. Baltimore: Messianic Jewish Publications, 2009.

Telushkin, Joseph. *Words That Hurt, Words That Heal*. New York: William Morrow, 1996.

Vermes, Geza. *Jesus in his Jewish Context*. Minneapolis: Fortress Press, 2003.

Wagner, Jordan. *The Synagogue Survival Kit*. Northvale, New Jersey: Jason Aronson Inc, 1997.

Whiston, William. *Josephus' Complete Works*. Grand Rapids: Kregel Publications, 1960.

Wright, N.T. *Paul and the Faithfulness of God*. Minneapolis: Augsburg Fortress, 2013.

124

INDEX

A

agape 61, 82, 118
ahavah 82
alcohol 87, 88
anger 76
anti-Semitism 32
apostle 65, 115
armor of God 106

C

cantillation 50
circumcision 30
conversion to Judaism 37

D

Dividing Wall 39, 40

E

evil speech 78

F

forgiveness 15, 80

G

gentiles i, iii, x, 2, 15, 17, 29, 30,
    31, 32, 37, 38, 39, 40, 41, 42,
    43, 45, 48, 50, 51, 52, 53, 55,
    59, 68, 71, 83, 118, 122
gifts of the Spirit 64
God-fearers 31, 39, 71

H

Haftarah 50
Holy Days 66

I

immersion 34, 63, 64, 95, 96
immersion of the Ruach 96
immorality 48, 73, 82

J

judgment 24, 25, 78

L

Lashon Ha-Ra 78
love 25, 30, 38, 44, 51, 55, 61, 62,
    67, 69, 70, 82, 87, 88, 94, 97,
    100, 117, 118

M

marriage 49, 82, 87, 91, 92, 93,
    94, 96, 97, 99
Mashiach ben David 26
Mashiach ben Yosef 26
M'chitzah 39, 51
Mikveh 34, 95, 96

N

Name of God 7, 63
Name of the Messiah 1, 19

O

Olam HaBa 26
Olam hazeh 23

P

Pidyon Ha-Ben 11
pornea 82
predestination 9
garments 86, 109, 110
Prophets 15, 44, 48, 50, 66, 91,
    119

R

rabbinic interpretation 41, 65, 86
Redemption of the First Born 11
Repairing the World 83
replacement theology 51
resurrection ix, 2, 25, 26, 42, 44,
    65, 95
Ruach HaKodesh 16, 79

S

Satan 23, 24, 105, 107, 108, 113
Shabbat 94
shaliach 2, 43, 48, 66, 117
speech 78, 79, 83, 87

T

teacher 35, 68, 69, 117
the age to come 19
this age 105
Tikkun Olam 83
Torah ix, xii, 1, 8, 10, 11, 13, 15,
    18, 19, 22, 23, 24, 34, 37, 41,
    48, 50, 55, 61, 66, 73, 74, 77,
    81, 82, 83, 84, 89, 91, 96, 101,
    102, 103, 109, 110, 113, 118,
    119
trope 50

U

unity 39, 42, 45, 51, 62, 63, 64

W

wedding 49, 95, 96, 97, 98
workplace 104
worship 39, 40, 53, 54, 56, 87, 88,
    89

Y

yetzer ha-ra/good inclinations 24 ,
    22, 75, 80, 83
yetzer ha-tov/evil inclinations 75,
    83